Moses Coit Tyler

Glimpses of England

social, political, literary

Moses Coit Tyler

Glimpses of England
social, political, literary

ISBN/EAN: 9783337071790

Printed in Europe, USA, Canada, Australia, Japan

Cover: Foto ©Suzi / pixelio.de

More available books at **www.hansebooks.com**

By Moses Coit Tyler

A History of American Literature during the Colonial Time. New Edition, revised, in two volumes. Volume I.—1607–1676. Volume II.—1676–1765. Each $2.50
Agawam edition, 2 vols. in one. $3.00

The Literary History of the American Revolution: 1763–1783. Two volumes, large octavo. Volume I.—1763–1776. Volume II.—1776–1783. Each $3.00

Three Men of Letters. Chapters in Literary Biography and Criticism Devoted to George Berkeley, Timothy Dwight, and Joel Barlow. 12° gilt top $1.25

Glimpses of England. Social, Political, Literary. 12°. . . . . . $

G. P. Putnam's Sons
NEW YORK AND LONDON

Moses Coit Tyler

Glimpses of England

SOCIAL
POLITICAL
LITERARY

BY

MOSES COIT TYLER

G. P. PUTNAM'S SONS
NEW YORK AND LONDON
The Knickerbocker Press
1898

Copyright, 1898
By
MOSES COIT TYLER
Entered at Stationers' Hall, London

To
EDMUND GOSSE
WITH THE GRASP OF A FRIENDLY HAND ACROSS THE SEA

PREFACE

THESE sketches have been selected from a very considerable number of the same sort written by me during a residence in England beginning with the year 1863 and ending with the year 1866.

No attempt is here made at being comprehensive or even systematic. I have chosen such papers as would justify the unpresuming title of the collection, by furnishing glimpses, at least, of a few of those aspects of English life, social, political, and literary, which the author himself looked at with deep interest while he was himself in the midst of it and felt for himself its strong and ardent pulse. I may add that the most of these papers originally appeared either in " The Nation " or in " The Independent."

Although the essays here brought together are not, either in direction or in method, just what I should now write from England or from any other country, this, I think, may fairly be said of them,—they are the honest testimony of a direct and a rather attentive observer, concerning some interesting men and some interesting things in England, at a very significant period of its recent history.

M. C. T.

Cornell University,
    1898.

CONTENTS

	PAGE
LONDON: SOME OF ITS ATTRIBUTES AND DIMENSIONS	1
JOHN STUART MILL AS A STUMP SPEAKER	13
MAZZINI	24
THE HON. AND REV. BAPTIST NOEL	33
MR. SPURGEON	42
JOHN STUART MILL IN THE HOUSE OF COMMONS	54
THE NEW REFORM MOVEMENT	64
MR. GLADSTONE IN DEFEAT	72
THE ACCUSATION AGAINST MR. GLADSTONE	82
THE HOUSE OF COMMONS:	
I. ITS LOCAL HABITATION	92
II. ITS PERSONAL COMPOSITION	102
III. ITS MANNERS	111
MR. DISRAELI	122
LORD BROUGHAM	137

	PAGE
EARL RUSSELL	144
JOHN BRIGHT:	
I. PERSONAL AND POLITICAL TRAITS	155
II. PHASES OF HIS CAREER	162
III. AS AN ORATOR	171
IV. AS AN ORATOR	182
V. AS AN ORATOR	191
HER MAJESTY THE QUEEN	200
THE HOME AND GRAVE OF COLERIDGE	216
A SUNDAY IN WALES	223
A PEEP AT THE CARDIFF CONSULATE	234
ENGLISH PLUCK	242
POPULAR LECTURING	253
ON CERTAIN ENGLISH HALLUCINATIONS TOUCHING AMERICA	277
AMERICAN REPUTATIONS IN ENGLAND	296

GLIMPSES OF ENGLAND

GLIMPSES OF ENGLAND

LONDON

SOME OF ITS ATTRIBUTES AND DIMENSIONS

HUGH MILLER relates how, after wandering about London for the first time and asking many questions of many people, he came to the conclusion that "Londoners do not know London"; and he playfully suggests that the great city, like certain great folks, has at last grown too big "for the familiarities of intimate acquaintance." But rather, it seems to me, is London like some many-sided and opulent soul that welcomes love, confidence, and even familiarity, but is unable in turn completely to reveal itself to any other soul, just because it can find none large enough and versatile enough to receive a revelation of the entire range of its faculties.

Indeed no mortal, cockney or otherwise, knows London; and it may be safely affirmed that until we shall have a race of men whose forte is what Sydney Smith said Macaulay's was, no mortal ever will know London. Even those astonishing persons, the cabmen and the policemen, who approach most nearly to Macaulay's specialty, and whose vocations compel them all their lives to a daily and nightly intimacy with the streets of the wondrous city, sometimes, after years of beating about the town, find themselves lost—to use a Hibernianism—and compelled to inquire the way among London streets which they then see for the first time.

And if no man can know London, neither can any man claim London. It disdains the audacity of special ownership, that it may give itself to mankind. It is for this reason, no doubt, that the foreigner in Great Britain often experiences a relief in passing from the larger provincial towns of the kingdom up to the metropolis. In Liverpool and Manchester he feels that he is on Englishmen's ground, in Glasgow and Edinburgh on Scotchmen's, but in London on his own. Like those pre-eminent personages in literature, art, or conduct, who outgrow the citizenship of any country and become fellow-citizens with all men, this city is no longer England's but the world's. It is cosmopolitan. Who of any nation is forbidden to salute the universal Shakespeare by the same

loving acclamation which John Milton used—
" my Shakespeare " ? And what countryman
under the sun, even though he be the celebrated
though ill-boding New Zealander of prophecy,
may not address the city on the Thames, as
Childe Harold did the city on the Tiber, with
the loyal strain,

" . . . my country, city of the soul " ?

And this claim on behalf of mankind for the
freedom of London, seems admitted by the
last report of that most absolute nineteenth-
century dogmatist, the census-taker, who,
among other curious facts, tells us that there
are more Scotchmen in London than in Edinburgh, more Irishmen than in Dublin, more
Germans than in any town of Germany excepting Berlin, more Roman Catholics than in
Rome, and more Jews than in Palestine.

In the present magnitude of London it is
amusing to remember the comments upon its
greatness made by Addison or Burke or Dr.
Johnson, at a time when it was to its present
self what the babe is to the man. One Good-
Friday, while Johnson and Boswell were trudg-
ing together along the Strand to attend service
at St. Clement Danes, Boswell remarked that
London was too large, for the reason " that
nobody was heeded by his neighbor,—there

was no fear of censure for not observing Good-Friday." The doctor quietly snubbed him for this pharisaical speech, but admitted that, for other reasons, London was really too large. It was then about one sixth its present size.

The growth of the town since the happy year when Londoners learned how, with proper accuracy, to count their own noses, presents a record full of interest to all men, and to us Americans in particular a record full of wholesome admonition on behalf of a grace rarely found in any part of the world—the grace of urban modesty.

In 1801 the population of London was.. 864,845
In 1811 it was........................ 1,009,546
In 1821 it was........................ 1,225,694
In 1831 it was........................ 1,474,069
In 1841 it was........................ 1,873,676
In 1851 it was........................ 2,363,141
In 1861 it was........................ 2,803,034

The tremendous meaning of these figures will not at first appear to one who simply gazes at them without some effort at comparison. Let us make that effort, for a moment.

In America our ears are often stunned by the din of exultation kept up at the growth of certain of our ambitious but still callow inland towns. The growth of these towns is indeed wonderful, but it would be none the less wonderful if there were somewhat less noise made about it. Who ever saw one rational Londoner exhibiting the least vanity at the amazing and pauseless increase of that titanic town? As soon would he think of finding food for individual conceit in the vastness of the solar system. Yet how the statistics of the expansion of London, which are left to tell in silence their own astounding tale, dwarf the local records of accumulating bulk which so many American citizens blazon at every corner and bellow from every housetop!

Taking the last census in each country as the standard of comparison, it appears that, during the ten years preceding 1861, London added to itself a new city one half the size of New York, more than twice the size of Baltimore, nearly three times the size of Boston, more than three times the size of Cincinnati or St. Louis, and more than four times the size of Chicago. If the eight cities of Buffalo, Rochester, Albany, Pittsburg, Newark, Providence, Portland, and Milwaukee had been taken up bodily in 1861, put on shipboard, conveyed across the Atlantic, and deposited on the fringe of the skirts of London, they, with their united populations, would not have added to London so much as London quietly added to itself during the previous decennial period. Every twelve months a new city springs into being along the globous verge of London equal to the entire city of Cleveland.

The author of the "Espriella Letters" divides the people of London into two races, the solar and the lunar. By some recent estimates it appears that these two races are now even more distinctly separated by the exactions of commerce, than they were in Southey's time by those of fashion. Several years ago the metropolis, like some enormous cyclops, was already sprawling out upon a couch of 78,000 acres; but the original city, the venerable parent of this gigantean monster, is still content with that pigmy bed of 723 acres on which it has reposed for a thousand years. The city, though so small, is still the centre of the trading, financial, and journalistic life of London, and has, it seems, a day population of 283,520 souls, and a night population of only 113,387 souls. Thus every morning there come rushing into the city from suburb and rural cottage and country villa, to toil and get rich within the narrow walls of the old city, 170,133 persons; while there are 509,611 customers and clients who enter the city every day to deal with them. What tremendous energy, then, must there be in the systole and diastole of this cyclopean heart, whose throb can suck in and expel every day along its veins and arteries a living stream of 679,744 human beings!

No Londoner, as we have already said, thinks of boasting of the awfully increasing proportions of London; but many a Londoner contemplates the subject with anxiety. One troublesome problem is that of ingress and egress. Every morning nearly a million of men make a rush to get into a space of seven hundred acres, and every night they make a rush to get out of it. No wonder that, in addition to streets on the level of the houses, they are compelled to build streets under the houses and streets over the houses, and that in a few years there must inevitably be three conterminous cities of London—terrene London, subterrene London, and superterrene London. But the swollen and congested state of the veins and arteries of the mighty town is not the only source of anxiety. What shall London do for lungs? A meeting was convened at the Mansion House some time ago, under the call of the lord mayor, to consider the peril arising from the disappearance of commons and of open spaces in the neighborhood of the metropolis. Mr. Thomas Hughes and other men of note addressed the meeting. The most important speech was embodied in some very startling and amusing estimates of the future development of London, presented by Mr. Benjamin Scott, the chamberlain of the city. He thought that, in dealing with the question before the meeting, they should not confine their calculations to 3,000,000 inhabitants. He found that in 1861 there were 3,222,717 persons living within an area of sixteen miles, taking Charing Cross as the centre. An increase of population had been going on within that area during the past half-century at the rate of nineteen per centum every ten years. In fifty years, at this rate, the population of the same area would be 8,532,000 souls. What would be their position fifty years hence, if they were allowed only the radius at present supposed to be sufficient? He found that in 1801 the several units of that population were twenty yards from one another, in 1851 about fourteen yards, and in 1866 something over nine yards. If this diminution of space went on for fifty years more, they would be more closely packed than his audience were at that moment; in fact, there would not be left even standing room for them.

We may get some impression of the present magnitude of London by looking at a few plain details of its colossal state. More than 350,000 houses are required for this giant to live in; and that he may take his walks and his drives with comfort, he has laid out and paved a number of streets which, if placed in line, would extend from Liverpool to New York. As he is not one of those good giants who go

early to bed, he has been obliged to erect for
his nocturnal delectation and guidance 360,000
gas-lamps along his streets, and to keep them
burning all night, thus consuming every twenty-
four hours about 13,000,000 cubic feet of gas.
To bathe his person, to wash his clothes, and
to supply the various vulgar needs of his
kitchen, as well as to furnish him occasionally
with a beverage which he is rather too much
inclined to despise, he uses 44,383,328 gallons
of water per day. He seems to depend a good
deal on artificial heat for a variety of purposes,
and is accordingly compelled to shovel into his
bin 5,000,000 tons of coal every year. Though
he does not always dress with great splendor,
his clothing bill is a generous one; for he constantly maintains 2950 merchant tailors, 3000
boot-and-shoe dealers, 1560 milliners and dress-
makers, and 1080 linen-drapers. Notwith-
standing the fact that he is endowed with
excellent locomotive faculties, he frequently
prefers to be carried, and for this purpose he
keeps always within call 5000 cabs, 1500 omni-
buses, and 24,000 horses, besides all the other
sorts of vehicles which human need can require
or human wit invent. Like giants in general,
he is blessed with a very tolerable appetite;
and as to thirst, it may be safely said that he is
never wholly free from its cravings. In the
course of every year he manages to devour

1,600,000 quarters of wheat, 240,000 bullocks, 1,700,000 sheep, 28,000 calves, 35,000 pigs, 10,000,000 head of game, 3,000,000 salmon, and innumerable fish of other sorts; while, during the same period, to use the language of one of our national humorists, he " puts himself outside " of 43,200,000 gallons of beer, 2,000,000 gallons of spirits, and 65,000 pipes of wine. His dairy may be regarded as a fairly respectable one, for he keeps 13,000 cows. It must be confessed that he does not altogether object to the vice nicotian, since he supports 1350 tobacconists. Of course any giant, whether Christian or pagan, who will go on eating, drinking, smoking, and otherwise rioting at this rate, to say nothing of his keeping his lamps burning all night, deserves to be ill; and we hear without surprise that he has provided himself with the constant attendance of 2400 medical men. To all his other qualities it is to be added that, though something of a rake and a good deal of a sot, he is in certain moods a marvellously religious giant, all which he proves by the fact that he maintains 852 churches and employs the ghostly counsel of 920 divines.

Such are a few outward aspects of London.—that province of bricks, that modern Babel of all lands and tongues—so well depicted by Walter Thornbury as " the vast, the negative, the miserable, the loathsome, the great, the magnificent." It is astonishing to consider how, by some unexplainable process which has been going on for a thousand years, this one small spot of earth has come to dominate the imaginations of men. The excellent Mrs. Slipslop, in Fielding's time, " always insisted on a deference to be paid to her understanding, as she had been frequently in London." That claim to superiority is a good one even yet. The Welsh lexicographer, William Owen, tells how, in the speech of his more rustic countrymen, London is always " the primary point in the geography of the world." The rustic conception seems not far removed from the cultivated one. That London is in some sense the world's summit and apex is properly announced in the universal phrase which describes every road thither as a road " up to London." Certainly, on no railway in this kingdom can there be any doubt as to the particular direction to be taken by what are called the " up-trains." I prefer to think of the pre-eminence of London in all the elements of physical greatness as but the expression of a spiritual pre-eminence which makes the British capital to-day the intellectual and moral capital of the globe. This seems, indeed, but another way of expressing assent to the opinion lately uttered by the American minister to Italy, that, " while other great cities represent individual nationalities, or restricted and temporary aims, the lasting, cardinal interests of universal humanity have their brightest point of radiation in the city of London."

1866.

JOHN STUART MILL AS A STUMP-SPEAKER

THE announcement that Mr. Mill was willing to enter the House of Commons, and that he would stand as candidate for Westminster, produced here a peculiar sensation, somewhat as if a being from the clouds were about to descend upon the London pavements, to be placarded against dead walls, to be bawled at in the streets, to be contradicted and hooted as he stood on the hustings. The effect of his great fame in letters and in philosophy, combined with his habit of personal seclusion, had been, so far as the public were concerned, to place him at the extremity of a long and rather sacred perspective. He seemed already on his pedestal among the immortals; and if Jeremy Bentham, or Adam Smith, or Bacon, or Aristotle, had been this year put in nomination for the British parliament, the immediate impression would have been not so very different.

At the outset of the canvass, there was an almost ludicrous difficulty in conveying to the worthy electors a conviction of Mr. Mill's personal actuality and tangibility. It was reported that he was just then in France; also, that he declined to come among them to solicit their votes. For them, his physical existence was necessarily a matter of mere faith; and as to any and every matter of mere faith, had not the ostensible writings of this alleged man done much to destroy the public respect for all such rubbish? By which one of the five senses of any ordinary elector of Westminster could the reality of the person of John Stuart Mill be verified ? They had, indeed, seen his printed signature—nothing more! Perhaps John Stuart Mill was not an incarnation at all; only a solemn, book-producing idea, vaguely localized for a part of the year in the neighborhood of Blackheath, every winter accustomed to evaporate in the direction of Avignon, incapable of being seen of fleshly eyes, even eluding all attempts at capture by the guileful photographer. In truth, Mr. Mill had all his life shunned crowds, had hated speech-making, had been a recluse—almost as much so as Tennyson. How, then, were the honest citizens of Westminster to be convinced that this four-lettered word, M-i-l-l, stood for anything more than a highly attenuated abstraction, and that its candidature for Westminster was not an adroit conspiracy of a learned but mischievous clique to get a seat in the house of commons for a pernicious system of morals or sociology? Finally, to not a few of the real pupils and friends of Mill, it did seem almost a profanation to have their august master the subject of a tumultuous and dirt-throwing political contest; and if successful, to have him—him whose writings were already quoted as authority in every great debate in parliament—brow-beaten there by some crass and arrogant Tory, or possibly out-talked and routed from the field by any glib insect of a politician.

I suppose that you have already had descriptions of the extraordinary contest which has just terminated so well. I am not to be intimidated by this consideration. The people of America cannot hear too much concerning our great friend,—one of the very few Englishmen of the highest eminence who, in the time of our agony, took the trouble to inform themselves as to the real facts of the case, and from first to last stood by us unflinchingly with intelligent approval, with faith, with hope, with good-will, and even with good advice. Therefore, whatsoever story others may have recently told you about him and about his nobly conducted and triumphant canvass, I must tell you my story too: at least I must give you my account of a tremendous mass-meeting of Mr. Mill's supporters which I attended, and where I saw and heard the philosopher himself on the stump.

It was the evening immediately preceding the polling day. Mr. Mill, having at last returned from his annual visit to the south of France, had been personally on the ground about ten days,—not to solicit votes, but to declare his opinions. The fight had become hot and furious. The very worst passions—those of theological prejudice and rancor—had been recklessly appealed to. On the one hand, as was said with compact and alliterative harshness, were bigotry, bribery, and beer; on the other, intelligent and reverent enthusiasm, unpaid and untiring work, a noble alarm lest England should be disgraced by the refusal of a seat in parliament to such a man as John Stuart Mill, finally the usual British determination to succeed in doing the thing undertaken. This meeting, which was appointed for St. Martin's Hall, Long Acre, was to be the last great demonstration before the battle. Reaching the place half an hour before the time designated, I found the great building already nearly full, with throngs pouring in at every entrance. As it seemed useless for me to try to make my way to the particular entrance to which my card invited me, I surrendered myself to the mighty current which was sweeping in through the principal door, and which thus bore me irresistibly into the middle aisle, and well up to the platform; where I became at once conscious of being securely planted in a fine standing situation of perhaps ten square inches, and enveloped by a dense mass of perpendicular and very determined Britons. Looking about as well as I could, I thought that I saw there an assemblage of uncommonly high quality both as to intelligence and as to moral force. For once, as it seemed to me, the rigid distinction of classes in England had here got broken up,—all the types in the huge form of English society having been at last, in St. Martin's Hall, thrown into pi. Jostling together in most admired disorder and propinquity were representatives of the working classes, of trade, of all the professions, with an obvious sprinkling of eager college students; while there was not lacking what, indeed, is usual at English political meetings, the presence of ladies on the platform and in the front seats. I do not think it could have been altogether a fancy of mine, but I thought I saw victory written on the faces of that buzzing multitude of Mr. Mill's supporters.

At last, and punctual to the minute, Mr. Mill, with his committee, emerged from a room at the back of the platform, and slowly made his way to the front. I shall not try to describe his reception. It was, indeed, for several minutes, a genuine tempest — a tempest of popular enthusiasm in the form of waving hats and handkerchiefs, of bodily commotion, and of acclamations that seemed to have the tremendous and peculiar ring not merely of lung power, but of heart power as well. Perhaps this last expression may seem to you somewhat mystical. Indeed, it seems so to myself; for I do not quite know how to convey to you the impression I got of certain rare moral elements — the sanctions of conscience, of enlightened thought, and of discriminating sympathy — which seemed to enter into, and to blend with, and to ennoble, these most vigorous physical demonstrations. At last, however, the tempest spent itself, and we were free to study the great man on whom the most of us then fixed our eyes for the first time.

He is, apparently, about five feet ten in height, of strong and rather angular frame, thin in flesh, bald, with a sharp, analytic face. His forehead is high but not broad. If I may quote the technical inventory of him, which a phrenological friend gave me, I would say that he has an immense development of the perceptives, of comparison, and of human nature, with less causality and ideality, and again with very large veneration and firmness. At any rate, even one who is not a phrenologist could see that his is a face and head exquisitely developed and spiritualized. It was, of course, a new experience for this bookish and cloistered man, this philosophical recluse, to be addressing a vast public meeting, and to be the object of these uproarious demonstrations of homage; but through the whole evening his self-command was perfect, the only external sign of agitation being in the flush upon his face, and a slight nervous twitching beneath the eyes during the frequent salvos of applause. I was informed that there were many well-known people on the platform; but the only faces that I was able to make out were those of the two French princes—the Duke d'Aumale and the Count de Paris—of Professor Masson, the biographer of Milton, and of our own Mr. Moncure Conway, who, with characteristic ardor, has been working for the election of two good Englishmen whom all good Americans love, to wit, Mr. Mill himself, and Mr. Thomas Hughes, just returned for Lambeth.

Of the speech which the philosopher made on this occasion, I shall not offer you even a synopsis. I will merely say that it was a massive, nobly simple, and lucid exposition of what he called "the great open question between capital and labor." As to the substance of his argument, is it not written in the chronicles of this man's studious and productive career,—particularly in his " Essays on Some Unsettled Questions of Political Economy," in his " Principles of Political Economy with Some Application to Social Philosophy," and in his " Dissertations and Discussions, Political, Philosophical, and Historical " ? I should like to add that his manner was that of quiet conversation; and that it was terse and brilliantly epigrammatic. He made not the least effort at anything in any way suggestive of oratory. He seemed like some venerable and benignant teacher, with his pupils sitting and standing about him by thousands, their heads strained forward in the attitude of persons unwilling that any syllable of that high, sweet, and thoughtful eloquence should be lost. The scene reminded one of the effect which Ben Jonson ascribes to the speaking of Bacon, whose " hearers could not cough, or look aside from him, without loss. He commanded where he spoke." Here was philosophy, not coldly dwelling apart from the common lot, but coming down into the market-place and the forum. It was fine to see the great thinker in the very act of addressing common men and women in mass-meeting, at the centre of the densest population of the metropolis; and putting before them in simple and most winning form the high and difficult ideas which of old would have been reserved for some literary aristocracy. It seemed to me, for one thing, that as a speaker he was ruled by a purpose like that of old Harington: "There is nothing in this world, next to the favor of God, I so much desire, as to be understood." I think Mill, at any rate, had his desire.

The address lasted about an hour. Then, as is the manly custom in English political meetings, came the time for questions in open court to the speaker, from anybody in the assemblage. In the present instance they were required to be in writing, and were passed up to the chairman, and were first read aloud by him. They seemed to range over nearly every topic that could possibly engage the attention of a British legislator; and Mr. Mill's replies, which he gave instantaneously upon hearing the questions, and with an indescribable look of pleasure, were in all respects most admirable,—candid, full, concise, luminous, pungent, practical. It struck me then, as never before, how great a mistake is made by those men who rush into public life without the most thorough scientific training,—without being educated for it, in short. After all, the human race is guided by philosophy. If our American political orators, for example, would prepare themselves for the service they are to undertake, by a study and mastery of fundamental principles, and then put them courageously into their speeches, they would find their audiences refreshed, kindled, and elevated by real ideas, as they never can be by story-telling, buffoonery, and bombast.

Suffer me, now, to finish this little history by incorporating into it a droll incident which occurred during the meeting, and very near to the spot where I was standing. A sturdy British citizen had, apparently, prepared himself for the great occasion by imbibing somewhat too freely of the national beverage. From the first, his political ardor, his yearning for utterance, seemed to be irrepressible. Even during Mr. Mill's speech, this excited patriot was scarcely prevented from interjecting fragments of his own intended address to the multitude. He shouted " Mr. Chairman," over and over again. He even tried to push his way to the platform; but he could no more move from his place than could a ship in the fatal hug of the Symplegades. At last, finding that he could not hope to proclaim his views from the platform, he resolved to unburden himself just where he stood, and accordingly he shouted, with the hiccoughing and the maudlin tones peculiar to men similarly inspired,— " Mr. Chairman, John—Stuart—Mill—is—a—fixed—fact! " The last two words were shot out with great force, and were received with roars of laughing applause; whereupon this prophet, thus delivered of his burden, straightway subsided into the arms of his fellow-electors just behind him. Afterward, as I wended my way home, musing upon this startling announcement of my inebriated neighbor at the meeting, I was inclined to regard it as but the stupid ebullition of a temporarily addled brain. On further consideration, however, I thought I saw a deep meaning in the poor man's speech. He had evidently been told that there was no such person as John Stuart Mill; that those words represented nothing but a shadow, an idea, an abstraction. He had come to the meeting in distress on that account,—a distress only partially relieved by the liquid consolations he had taken in by the way. At last, however, he had been permitted to behold this remarkable abstraction; he had heard it talk; he had seen it sit down, and stand up, and walk about; consequently he wished to declare to his fellow-citizens his deep joy on having been able to ferret out another Tory lie, by the discovery that John Stuart Mill was something more than a fleeting shadow or a fiction,—was, in short, " a fixed fact." Happily for them, for England, for the credit of the age, a sufficient number of the electors of Westminster showed the next day that they had made the same discovery.

21 July, 1865.

MAZZINI

A FEW days ago there appeared in a Paris newspaper the following somewhat sensational paragraph:

"Joseph Mazzini is at this moment ill in an humble dwelling in Brompton Road. The man who for so long was the incarnation of Italian unity expires in the fogs of the north, and in a climate which kills him. Now that the old conspirator no longer is in a position to terrify anyone, why does not the King of Italy allow him to breathe his last on his native soil?"

On authority which is simply perfect I am able to state that the case is not quite so bad as this writer puts it. Let not the melodramatic reference to the "humble dwelling in Brompton Road" lead anyone to suppose that in Mazzini's situation and circumstances there is anything of destitution. The house in which he lodges is not a palace, but it is a good, respectable dwelling, such as most literary men and artists occupy; and Brompton itself is one of the pleasantest parts of London, peculiarly genial for persons of weak lungs, and for many generations a favorite place of residence for intellectual people. In that neighborhood in olden time lived Sir Thomas More and Sir Isaac Newton; and in recent date, Turner, Thomas Carlyle, Thackeray, Sothern, Boucicault, the sculptor Baron Marochetti, and many other persons of note. I believe Mazzini has no private fortune; but among the intellectual aristocracy of every land he has the most devoted friends, who are proud to enable this tireless man to pursue his wonderful career. He lives with a dignified and philosophic simplicity, reminding one of Beranger. With regard to Mazzini's health, his nearest friends here have, during the past few weeks, felt great anxiety. It is true he is only fifty-six years of age; but few men of any epoch have gone through so much labor, excitement, study, and disappointment. He is physically one of the little great men of history. He is very short, slender, emaciated; his hair and whiskers, which must once have been a luxuriant black, are now very gray. His face is one of the noblest and sweetest that was ever lighted up by thought and love; and now, deeply marked with lines of study, anxiety, and years, it is a face so spiritual and so pure that one is drawn to it by an irresistible charm.

It is the face at once of a hero and a martyr, of a philosopher and a saint. The eyes are of the genuine Italian jet, but their deep, fiery intensity is tempered by the gentleness and benignity of the indwelling soul. Altogether —in face, manner, conversation, as well as in the historic and somewhat mysterious associations which surround his person—there are all the elements of that extraordinary fascination by which this great man has during so long a period bound to himself and the cause of liberalism so many of the best spirits of all lands. For several years he has been engaged in collecting and revising his writings; and, in addition to this work, the unresting laborer for human liberty carries on an immense correspondence with reformers in many nations; he keeps his eye jealously fixed on all the great political movements of the world; and silently and ceaselessly into all lands go the letters of Mazzini, to guide, to stimulate, to moderate, and to inspire his political pupils; and the soul of Mazzini reappears in countless lectures, orations, editorial articles, and state papers. Probably no other man now living spends more hours every day over his desk. As he takes no exercise, and almost no nourishment, these labors must naturally be telling upon him; and, though we may all hope that the picture of his physical state drawn by the writer in the

French paper is an exaggeration, there is evident ground for alarm.

The city of Genoa, which gave Christopher Columbus to the world, is likewise the native place of Mazzini. There he was born in 1809. His father was a physician and a medical professor at the University of Genoa. At that university, also, Joseph received his education. From his youth he took a passionate interest in the welfare of his countrymen; and brooding over the political degradation of Italy, he early consecrated himself to the mission of awakening its political life, with the hope, which he still refuses to abjure, of founding Italian unity on the basis of a republic. While still very young he established "The Genoa Indicator," which we may well believe was a somewhat radical newspaper. He soon allied himself with that celebrated and terrible secret society, the Carbonari; and his reason for this step he has given in the following words, which I quote for their illustration both of his personal history and of his fine English style:

"I was at that time unable to set up any association of my own; and in the Carbonari I found a body of men in whom—however inferior they were to the idea they represented—thought and action, faith and works, were identical. Here were men who, defying alike excommunication and capital punishment, had the persistent energy ever to recommence and weave a fresh web each time the old one was broken ; and this was enough to induce me to join my name and my labors to theirs."

For this he was imprisoned in the fortress of Savona for six months; he was then tried and acquitted, but sent into exile. He went to Marseilles, where he founded another Italian paper, in the same spirit as the one just broken up. By the government of Louis Philippe he was soon ordered to quit France ; but for another year he succeeded in eluding the police and in printing his paper, each issue of which was carried by swift hands into Italy. At length, in 1833, he went to Switzerland and organized the expedition into Savoy, which failed through the treachery of Ramorino. Compelled to flee from Switzerland, he reached London in 1837, where he has lived, with many interruptions, for nearly thirty years. He went hard to work with his pen; he established a school and a newspaper. In the convulsions of 1848, Mazzini was again upon the continent and became the leading spirit of the Roman republic ; but on its failure he returned to London. In 1857 he made another unsuccessful expedition—this time to revolutionize Naples. He has no faith in the kingdom of

Italy. In early life he became a democrat; he then labored to unite the Italians in a republic; and he still lives as if he constantly applied to himself the message of the dying marquis in Schiller's " Don Carlos ": " Tell him that when he is a man, he must reverence the dreams of his youth."

The first time I saw Mazzini and listened to his conversation, I wondered at the slender form, the pale, thin face, and the gentle words of a man usually represented as a flaming and ferocious demagogue, conspirator, and revolutionist; and I thought, Can this be he at whose fiery heart millions have drunk inspiration, whose slightest word has caused kings to shake amid their myrmidons, whose counsels have made all Europe rock to its centre? Can this frail and sweet-voiced man be the terrible Enceladus couched beneath the Ætna of European politics, at whose turnings the volcano has heaved with fearful convulsions, and belched forth the hot lava of revolution? Arrayed wholly in black, his coat closely buttoned to the chin, he moved and looked rather like some timid denizen of a cloister, like some meek, lettered, university professor, than that remorseless monster of unrest—of plotting, of regicide, and of tumult—which he is usually painted. Far back in the depths of those wonderful eyes, however, one could imagine the reserved fire of the giant to be slumbering—not slumbering either, but watching and waiting with that eternal vigilance which is the price of liberty.

Probably a more absolutely fearless man than Mazzini cannot be imagined. For thirty years and more, while the police of Europe have been watching for him, while kings have been moving earth and hell for his capture, he has gone back and forth over the continent beneath their very noses. It is generally supposed that Mazzini is a great master of disguises. He himself told me that, during the most of his career, he has gone wheresoever he has desired hither and thither across Europe, without any disguise at all — travelling publicly, in his ordinary dress, like any private gentleman. Doubtless this saved him. The police were on the watch for a man travelling mysteriously. It is like the first Lord Stanhope, who affirmed that he always misled the diplomatists by just telling them the naked truth. But Mazzini's fearlessness extends beyond the realm of police interference; he has never had the slightest fear of cholera or any other pestilence, but goes and stays where duty leads, though it be into the heart of a plague-smitten metropolis.

Without lifting the veil which rightly covers the sacred scenes of domestic privacy, perhaps it may not be improper for me to refer to an incident of a very touching character, which reveals another side of Mazzini's nature—his tenderness and love for children. It was on an exquisitely beautiful day in August, and in a quiet, rural cemetery on the face of a hill a few miles north of London, that an English family, with a few of their nearest kindred and friends, stood with uncovered heads around a little grave, into which was being laid the lifeless body of a sweet child. Mazzini was there, an honored and a beloved friend. He had held that little child on his knee, had played with her, had parted her golden hair over her forehead. After the prayer of the minister, and after the nearest kindred had taken their final look into the grave, I saw Mazzini stand there still gazing upon it, the tears coming thick and fast from his eyes; and then, brushing them aside, the sad-looking, lonely man walked slowly away. It was difficult to think of him as the hardiest, the most resolute and tempestuous spirit in Europe. The terrible old conspirator shedding tears over the grave of a sweet little English girl presented a picture of genuine pathos and of profound suggestiveness. No one would have loved him the less for it, or have admired him the less. Nay, it was the crowning proof of his heroic nature.

How more fittingly can this letter close than by reminding you of the recent words of Mazzini concerning America, in his noble letter to Moncure Conway:

"You have abolished slavery. You have as a crowning to your glorious struggle decreed that the sun of the republic shines on all; that he who breathes the air of the republic is free; that as God is one, so on the blessed soil where liberty is not a hap-and-hazard fate, but a faith and a gospel, the stamp of mankind is one. Can you mutilate this great principle? Can you cut it down to the monarchical half-freedom standard? proclaim the existence of the half-man? constitute in the republican American land a middle-ages class of political serfs? Is there liberty without the vote?"

Perhaps those sad Italian eyes penetrate farther into the meaning and the mystery of events which are now in agitation in America than many another's which gaze at those events from a nearer point of view, but amid the blinding drapery of the storm.

9 January, 1866.

THE HON. AND REV. BAPTIST NOEL

MANY years ago the upper spheres of English society were invaded by the startling announcement that a new popular preacher, belonging to a family of noble rank, had made his appearance in London, and was attracting and delighting vast audiences. From the days of Peter the fisherman, of Luther the miner's boy, of Whitefield the son of a tavern-keeper, to those of Edward Irving and Charles Spurgeon, the great popular preachers of the world have commonly sprung from poor cradles, and have made their ways onward among men without the help of the least purple in the blood. "Poor mechanics," saith William Penn, "are wont to be God's great ambassadors to mankind." But here had uprisen a popular preacher who was certainly not a plebeian. Born in the year 1799, educated at Trinity College, Cambridge, a son of Sir Gerald Noel-Noel and of the Baroness Barham, a brother of the Earl of Gainsborough, and a pulpit orator of such gifts that crowds everywhere followed him, the Hon. and Rev. Baptist Wriothesley Noel set forth upon his career with advantages such as are rarely combined in one person. Taking human nature as we find it, and especially the English compartment of human nature, we may easily believe that the aristocratic origin of the preacher brought him into notice much more rapidly than even his talents could have done had he been the son of nobody. For, as a sparkling English writer has candidly remarked, " Next in estimation in this great country to a real live lord is a real live lord's relative. If you cannot shake hands with a real peer, it is something to shake hands with his brother." Certainly, had Baptist Noel been an ambitious man, there was no distinction in the English establishment which he might not have hoped to attain. But they who went to hear the aristocratic young divine instantly discovered that he was not an ambitious man. Nay, though a genuine pulpit orator, he seemed to be not even ambitious of pulpit oratory. Every word, look, tone, movement, the whole spirit of his thought and utterance, denoted a preacher of absolute self-forgetfulness, absorbed and concentrated, as " beneath the Great Taskmaster's eye," upon the one purpose of doing good to mankind. Tall, erect, graceful, with a countenance of peculiar beauty and benignity, with a chastened and eloquent diction, and an imagination, though evidently kept in check, often flashing irresistibly in some brilliant image that revealed the poetry still alive in his Noel blood, he preached like one who wished his hearers not to think of the preacher, but of the preacher's theme. No homiletical claptrap, no straining for outward effect, no attempt at wit or rhetorical decoration interfered with the solemn and transparent simplicity of his discourse. He was of the low church and evangelical party; and in his sermons he rigorously held himself to the enforcement of the most pungent and undiluted Calvinism. The results attending such preaching by such a man may be easily imagined.

He became a power in London and a person of vast prestige and influence throughout the kingdom. St. John's Chapel, Bedford Row, of which he was minister, was always thronged; and the members of his church became distinguished as among the most laborious in all the great religious and philanthropic tasks of the day. Mr. Noel himself was indefatigable in working for the city missions, in seeking to gain the attention of the young men of London, in all measures for the rescue of fallen women, and in whatever seemed likely to diminish poverty, and profligacy, and wretchedness in the squalid caverns of the metropolis. He was appointed chaplain to the Queen, and in his turn preached in the royal chapels of St. James and Whitehall. It is said that a bishopric was repeatedly offered to him, and declined; but whether this be so or not, there can be no doubt that the offer of one was merely a matter of time.

Such were the outward tokens of influence and success, when, in 1848, he quietly and solemnly announced to the world that he could no longer remain in the Established Church. They whose recollections extend to that year cannot have forgotten the shock and commotion produced by this announcement throughout the Protestant world: on the one hand, amazement, rage, disgust; on the other, jubilant welcome, congratulation, and delight. An American needs to come to England and stop a while in order to appreciate the tremendous social prestige of the Established Church, and, consequently, the depth of conviction and of heroism required by any man, especially a man with such personal alliances, to go out from its fellowship, and cast in his lot with the dissenters. To some his proceeding seemed mere lunacy, to others high treason, to others abominable wilfulness and perversity. The Church batteries opened upon him their fiercest broadsides of abuse; pre-eminently, that newspaper which was then the organ of the evangelicals, feeling most the hurt of the rupture, kept hot for many months, against this gentlest and meekest of men, its artillery of denunciation, even as it has since done in the case of Frederick Robertson, gashing and rending his heart while living, and stamping its vituperation upon his grave. But, on the part of the great, free, intelligent non-conformist body of England, the cordiality of his reception fully equalled in intensity the fury of those from whom he had withdrawn; and in the presence of an immense assemblage, presided over by Rowland Hill's successor, and amid devotional exercises and addresses of thrilling interest, Mr. Noel was fittingly received into the ranks of dissent.

He then gave to the world his celebrated " Essay on the Union of Church and State "; illustrating with fidelity, precision, and masterly logic his conception of the great evils of such a connection. In the following year he published his " Essay on Christian Baptism," and once more surprised the public, and probably disappointed the Congregationalists, by uniting himself with the Baptist denomination—becoming pastor of the congregation near his former charge, over which he has remained ever since. Although here and there in society one still hears him spoken of with asperity as a clerical turncoat and deserter, the public fight against him has long since raved itself to rest. And happily enough, when two years ago Mr. Spurgeon, in his impassioned sermon entitled " Baptismal Regeneration," made his vehement onslaught upon the Established Church, Baptist Noel had the opportunity, and took it with a sweet joy, of acting as a pacificator; he stood forth with great effect between the brethren he had left and the brethren he had joined—nobly vindicating the former, firmly chiding the latter, and breathing upon both a spirit of Christian forbearance and peace.

The first time I ever saw Baptist Noel was shortly after my arrival in London three years ago, at a great meeting in Finsbury Chapel, called to hear Sella Martin and Moncure Conway on the American question. Mr. Noel presided. It is one of his extraordinary qualities that, while he regards himself as simply an evangelist, and is almost incessantly engaged in preaching revival sermons, he has the head and the heart and the time to watch minutely the political struggles of humanity in all parts of the world, and to form his judgments upon great crises as they arise; not, as many English people did in our extreme agony, by the good old swallowing process out of the great nurse-spoon of a hostile daily press, but independently and from original investigation. No one in America needs to be told that Baptist Noel was one of our earliest, most pronounced, and most constant champions. On the occasion to which I refer he opened the meeting with a half-hour's speech. I had been in England just long enough to find how much the average Englishman knew of the merits of our struggle, and with what emphasis, flippancy, and disdain he had decided our national destiny and damnation. That night almost for the first time (not quite the first time, for I had already spent two or three hours with George Thompson) I saw an Englishman who had a perfect and minute knowledge of our country, its geography, its public men, its great parties, and those minor and finer shades of political distinction which are in themselves so important, and yet for a stranger so difficult to grasp. His speech was lucid, comprehensive, and unanswerable; and in the acquaintance it displayed with the interior structure of a distant nation which he had never visited, it was wonderful.

I have since several times heard him at public meetings and in his own chapel. At the latter there is no crowd nor excitement, but a large congregation of middle-class people, who listen with reverence to the solemn teachings of their venerable pastor, and are instructed by him in the great Christ-like art of practical work. Baptist Noel tolerates no idlers or dawdlers; if people come to his chapel, they have to do something; and he has built up one of the most indefatigable working congregations in London. It cannot be doubted that, so far as the present age is concerned, his influence has been lessened by his withdrawal from the Established Church. There is not the éclat about his name which there used to be. Strangers can now do what they could not have done twenty years ago—they can visit London without hearing Baptist Noel. The very building in which he used formerly to minister had a sort of historical eminence: it was erected for the clerical demagogue Sacheverel; Scott, the commentator, was once its curate; there Cecil preached, and Daniel Wilson, afterward bishop of Calcutta; there Wilberforce worshipped, and occasionally brought with him his illustrious friends Pitt, Burke, and others. Judged by external considerations, it was a great descent from this renowned chapel to a plain, nameless, fameless Baptist conventicle.

Mr. Noel's published writings are very numerous. I find that the mere titles of his books cover fourteen pages of the catalogue of the British Museum. The mention of some of them will give one a fair idea of the versatility of his knowledge and the universality of his sympathies: "Africa and the East," "The Christian Sabbath," "Evils Produced by Late

Hours of Business," "The Free Church of Scotland," "Visit to the Valley of Piedmont," "Progress of the Gospel in France," "The Church of Rome," "The Corn Laws," "The Fallen and their Associates," "The Fight between Sayers and Heenan," "Infant Piety," "Protestant Thoughts in Rhyme," "Freedom and Slavery in the United States," "A Town in Switzerland," "The Rebellion in America."

Mr. Noel is also the author of many hymns, some of them of rare delicacy, pathos, and beauty; and I will close this sketch by quoting a few verses from one which very well reveals his characteristics as a hymn-writer:

> "There's not a bird with lonely nest
> In pathless wood or mountain crest,
> Nor meaner thing, which does not share,
> O God, in Thy paternal care.
>
> There's not a being now accurst
> Who did not taste Thy goodness first;
> And every joy the wicked see
> Received its origin from Thee.
>
> Each barren crag, each desert rude,
> Holds Thee within its solitude;
> And Thou dost bless the wanderer there
> Who makes his solitary prayer.
>
> In busy mart and crowded street,
> No less than in the still retreat,
> Thou, Lord, art near, our souls to bless
> With all a parent's tenderness."

30 March, 1866.

MR. SPURGEON

IN his vast Tabernacle, at the seething centre of a dense population of London artisans, shop-keepers, and day-laborers, Mr. Spurgeon preaches to the largest Protestant congregation in the world. His portrait has been so many times drawn, especially by my own countrymen and for them, that I shall not here elaborately attempt it. I wish merely to give some results of my own observations on the spot as to the chief elements of his present amazing power,—a power derived in part from his own qualities, in part from the great outward position which he has at last achieved.

First of all, the approach to his Tabernacle, though it takes one through a grimy and foul-smelling district, is yet very impressive to a stranger. If you go thither, as you should do, on the top of an omnibus, you are set down at the "Elephant and Castle," and you stand amazed in a space into which seven great thoroughfares are constantly pouring their streams of hurrying life; and presently your eye rests upon Mr. Spurgeon's vast edifice, with its imposing array of columns in front; and you are reminded of a thing which signifies a great deal here, that Spurgeon's Tabernacle is an established affair, and, like St. Paul's, the Tower, and Westminster Abbey, is one of the greatest and most substantial things of this greatest and most substantial city of the planet. Everybody feels that the man who at the age of twenty-seven could have called together such a tremendous mass of stones, and who could have piled them up in such a shape, is himself no sham, no ephemera, but a reality and a power.

That such is the general conclusion, needs no better proof than is furnished by the present attitude of his ministerial brethren towards him. During the earlier years of his career in London, while the boy, Charles Spurgeon, was still in the thick of the fight for recognition, and really had some little use for a few influential friends, there rained upon his defiant young head, from all the batteries of the dissenting clergy, one long storm of shot and shell in every shape of denunciation, ridicule, and whispered scandal, envy-born and remorseless. With some exceptions, beautiful but few, his clerical brethren made a point of snubbing him and cutting him upon all possible occasions. For example, the Rev. ——, the model of a showy, pliant, sleek, and sumptuous city pastor, frowned majestically upon the rising, but still unrecognized luminary of Exeter Hall; and, on one occasion, having promised to preach in the evening at the dedication of a certain chapel, withdrew his presence with unctuous indignation on learning that Mr. Spurgeon was to preach in the same place in the morning. But now—how changed! All this sort of treatment has become a thing of the past; and the late authors of it would gladly have the word " past ", with reference to that chapter of personal history, synonymous with the word " oblivion." Mr. Spurgeon is now an indisputable success. And it is a quite notable fact that since his removal into his vast stone Tabernacle, these same magnanimous divines, not exactly

> " True as the dial to the sun
> Although it be not shined upon,"

have proved themselves to be more than willing to salute the risen sun, and to warm and exhibit themselves by his light.

But if the sight of Spurgeon's enormous church gives you an impression of a certain personal power in the very young man you are going to hear, that impression is at once intensified by your gliding into the huge crowd which passes through the doors, and then beholding that always wonderful spectacle — seven thousand human beings filling every space in the vast temple, filling the body of the room, the aisles, the platform, and the galleries—galleries rising to the very roof all around the room. Few heads are cool enough to help being awed, excited, exhilarated by a scene so sublime. I used to think that, if a student of grammar could not comprehend the meaning of a noun of multitude, he should be sent for one Sunday to Plymouth Church in Brooklyn; but when I went to the Metropolitan Tabernacle, I opened a new cell of appreciation concerning that phrase of grammar. Certainly, these are some capital elements of strength in this man's position. He who has once gained such a vantage-ground fights the battle henceforward with all the odds in his favor. Before Mr. Spurgeon comes to his audience, his audience are already conciliated, keyed up to expectancy, and in a magnetic state largely submissive to the tempestuous tyranny of his eloquence. There is a grand strategy in eloquence, as in war; the speaker's spiritual position toward his audience is as important as the soldier's physical one toward his foe; and the one speaks, as the other fights, with great disadvantage if the sun is in his face, a morass in front of him, with steep hills just beyond.

At exactly the appointed moment, Mr. Spurgeon descends upon the platform—quiet, self-possessed, with an earnest purpose written in his look, perfectly assured of victory. What are his chief attributes ? To begin with, there is his voice. Without the least apparent effort on the part of him who emits it, it fills all the room, it fills every ear, with its delicious amplitude and sweetness of sound. It is a wondrous gift, that voice of Spurgeon's—rich, full, satisfying. You would travel far to hear such a voice. I frankly confess that, in the several times that I have heard him, he has not said one thing which in itself greatly impressed me; yet I listened with delight to the evolution of that grand vocal power of his, my thoughts following the play of its intonations along sentences whose meaning was too drearily commonplace for attention. His next personal advantage is his personal appearance. This, I am aware, is contrary to the general notion. It is often said that his looks are against him. It is a mistake. It is true, he is not handsome, his appearance is not intellectual; but he is stout and broad; he has a broad face, broad shoulders, a broad body; he is a solid, capacious Briton, and that fact carries literally great weight. I do not know whether Spurgeon be tall; but he is big, and bigness is a most important condition of success in this land. It is with the English preacher very much as it is with the English dowager, who, according to Hawthorne, "impresses awe and respect by the muchness of her personality." And I have seen this view distinctly supported by one of the denominational papers of London; which declares, in so many words, that the preachers most worthy of honor are men of great girth of waist; and even adds that it is difficult to put the same amount of confidence in the slender divine as will naturally be reposed in his stouter brother. It seems to be an amiable trait of the British character to reverence the man of adipose achievements, and to infer that he who can heroically assimilate roast beef and beer can do almost anything. But if a man have not breadth, he must at least make up for it by having length. The most damaging point which "Punch" makes against Earl Russell is by letting the people know that he is little. If he could contrive to grow six inches, his ministry would last considerably longer than it is now likely to do. When Garibaldi was here, everybody tried to see him and to shake hands with him. The police guarded the approach to Stafford House. The little fellows, who had no introductions, had to stand back. But a great-bodied Canadian whom I knew, who had no introduction, stalked like a stately bishop up to the very door, the policemen standing back to give him room, while the flunkies, awestruck, passed him into the very presence of Garibaldi.

Spurgeon's next strong point is his fluency. It is impossible to conceive anything more facile than his utterance. I have it from one who heard his first sermon, when he came up to London in 1853, a raw country youth of nineteen, that this wonderful ease and flow of speech was the quality in him which first struck them. And it is not mere volubility—an abnormal and senseless mouthing of articulate wind; it is a genuine gift of swift, never-failing, well-chosen speech. I never heard from him an ungrammatical or a bungling sentence, or even a misplaced word. His language is pure Saxon. This is indeed a conspicuous source of his power with the common people—he talks their language. He is often accused of vulgarisms. The accusation is a compliment. It is an accusation which has been made against the great orators of all ages, Demosthenes, Chatham, Patrick Henry, Luther, Latimer, Knox, Whitefield, Henry Ward Beecher; it simply means that Spurgeon is one of those exceedingly rare men who have the sense and the courage, even in theology, to call a spade a spade, and not an oblong horticultural implement, and hell, hell, not the place of igneous sulphuric and fumiferous torment. A courtly preacher of the last century was lamenting to old Daniel Burgess his want of success. "Thank your velvet mouth for that—too fine to speak market language," was old Daniel's reply. Spurgeon is never guilty of this weakness. He gives to the people the Everlasting Gospel in the vernacular of Newington Butts.

Next, he is precisely fitted to get hold of his hearers by his thorough common-sense, by his ability to put everything in a practical, businesslike British way, without any idealization, dreaminess, or troublesome profundity; and, above all, by a quaint, hearty humor which tinges and flavors every discourse. "Why," said he one day, when urging upon his hearers the duty of individual effort, without depending on organizations and committees, "if the Lord had given the building of Noah's ark into the hands of a committee, it would not have been finished yet." Again, speaking of the toil of preaching, he once said, "I sometimes tell my brethren, when they complain that preaching is hard work, that it is indeed hard work to preach twice a week; but when you begin to preach twelve times a week, then it comes easy." One week-day, after preaching at a chapel in the country, he stood alone for a few minutes, and seemed likely to be left without an invitation to dinner. Presently a minister of the village came to him and said,

"I can't make out, Brother Spurgeon, when you study. When do you, now, get time to make your sermons?" "Oh, I'm always studying. I am sucking in something from everything. If you were to ask me home to dine with you, I should suck a sermon out of you."

But after all, and above all, the grand secret of Spurgeon's power is his obvious and total consecration to the one work which he feels himself called to attend to: it is that magnetic, overwhelming, victorious something which men call earnestness. Every one of Spurgeon's seven thousand hearers feels that there stands before him one real man, if there be no other in the world; a man who may be narrow, coarse, and in many things mistaken, but who is absolutely sincere, and who desires, above all things, to do men good. This, indeed, is the highest eloquence—the eloquence of character. I suppose that most persons could give the same reason for their going to hear Spurgeon, which Sheridan gave for going to hear Rowland Hill: "I go to hear Rowland Hill because his ideas come red-hot from his heart." A gentleman on a visit to John Bacon's studio, paused a long time before the bust of Whitefield: "After all that has been said, he was a great man; he was the founder of a new religion." "A new religion, sir?" said Bacon.

"Yes," said the visitor; " what do you call it ?" " Nothing but the old religion revived with new energy, and treated as though the preacher meant what he said." That last sentence of the sculptor's is, perhaps, the ultimate explanation of the transcendent success of Spurgeon.

On the other hand, probably most educated persons who go to hear him, while surprised at the absence of those eccentricities of manner and of that coarseness in speech which he used to have, think it wonderful that he can hold his position by sermons so utterly commonplace, invariably cast, also, in the textual mould, which, as Dr. Bethune has said, is "little better than tricky conceit"; by sermons so destitute of intellectual freshness, so narrow in their deduction and direction, so positive, so dogmatical, so wanting in appreciation of honest doubt, so sternly unwilling to make allowance for real difficulties with the problems of life. In another view, however, this latter fact is but another element of success. There are many men in the ministry who as preachers would far surpass Spurgeon, if it were not for the fact that they cannot get their minds thoroughly made up on two or three matters of doctrine. Hamlet would never have built the Metropolitan Tabernacle.

It is not strange that the English admirers of Mr. Spurgeon should be fond of asking an

American visitor how their great pulpit orator compares with ours. I, for one, always reply, that it is hardly fair to institute a comparison between two preachers, so great, indeed so wonderful, and yet so different, as are Charles Spurgeon and Henry Ward Beecher. If, however, the comparison be insisted on, it seems to me to amount to such parallel and contrast as every one must easily perceive between a single trumpet, played stirringly and heard afar, yet with a range of effect necessarily narrow, and a full-powered orchestral band, directed by the wand of genius, enriching all listeners with the most varied opulence of thought, sentiment, and sound.

One word, as I conclude, on Spurgeonism. Silently, but rapidly, within the pale of this great Baptist sect in England, and covering all the land with its network of moral power, there is being formed a distinct body of Spurgeonite preachers—energetic young men, trained in Spurgeon's college, imbued with Spurgeon's intense spirit, copying with an unconscious but ludicrous fidelity even the minutiæ of Spurgeon's manner of speech, proud of their connection with Spurgeon's name, and in constant communication with the great famous Spurgeonite head centre in London. At one time, just after his secession from the Evangelical Alliance, Mr. Spurgeon seemed to be gradually separating himself from the general organization of the religious world and even of the Baptist denomination, and to be concentrating all his force upon his immense congregation, his college, and the many churches which, throughout the kingdom, have taken his pupils for pastors; and until a very recent date it was not uncommon to hear leading Baptist ministers express in private the belief that, in the course of the next twenty years, Spurgeonism, having become a vast organic and wondrously vitalized body, might set up as a distinct sect under the name and banner of its founder. Mr. Spurgeon, however, with a noble warmth, has protested against such a tendency; and has lately taken measures, in concert with his clerical brethren, to signalize his close and indissoluble union with the Baptist denomination. Perhaps he prefers to be remembered as a Whitefield, rather than as a Wesley,—if, indeed, it be not too great a compliment to Whitefield to intimate such a resemblance between him and Spurgeon. Surely, in the preacher's power of holding his own before the same congregation with increasing effect for many years, and in the statesman's power of organizing beneficent ideas into permanent institutions, Spurgeon at thirty-one is already a greater man than Whitefield ever was, though he lived to the age of fifty-six.

March, 1866.

a financier were capable of assuming; Mr. Mill, at the upper end of one of the Independent Liberal benches immediately behind the place of John Bright, conspicuous for the innovation of keeping his hat under the bench instead of upon his head, and for his noble, pure, intellectual face always turned attentively towards the member who may be speaking, and reflecting, as in some exquisite and sensitive mirror, whatever worthy thought or emotion may be generated by the debate.

The first important subject which came before Parliament this year happened to involve one in which Mr. Mill is the great authority, that of economics; and he but yielded to the general expectation in making his maiden speech without that probation of silence to which parliamentary catechumens usually submit. The cattle plague was to be stamped out. Veterinary science had broken down. The pole-axe alone remained — the last argument of butchers. Every beast guilty of infection was to be instantly killed. But the great agricultural interest, never very eloquent and never very bashful, demanded that the government should compensate the owners for all cattle thus sacrificed.

"Not so," was substantially the reply of Mr. Mill; "let the farmers as a class organize among themselves a fund for the compensation of individual losers belonging to their class; since the farmers as a class, by the increase in the price of beef in proportion to the diminution of supply, are, according to inevitable economic laws, to be fully compensated for the aggregate loss. But if government shall pay for every beast killed, the farmers will be paid twice over, and the general body of the community will have to pay twice over, first by the extra taxation, and secondly by the extra price of beef."

When Mr. Mill rose, there was a movement of respectful attention throughout the whole House. The great economist whose writings had been quoted there for years was at last present to speak for himself. His physical organization is of that fine and delicate sort which, with reference to the indwelling spirit, may be said to be almost transparent; and on this his first appearance his bearing was so diffident yet so sincere, so tremulous yet so intensely earnest, with so much of the reality of a great intellectual authority, yet so free from the slightest assumption of it, that the genuine English courtesy of the House was conciliated into a deferential and really applausive silence. Almost the only fault in his speech was one easily remedied: his voice, probably from nervous agitation, was pitched in too feeble a key. The essential and the gratifying thing indicated by that first speech was his ability to think acutely and profoundly on his legs and in the midst of a multitude, and the power of clothing his thought tersely and fluently in the choicest words. Two nights after, Mr. Ayrton, —member for George Thompson's old constituency, the Tower Hamlets,—a glib lawyer who considers himself foreordained to speak on all possible subjects and who is never guilty of any excess of self-depreciation, indulged in a fling at Mr. Mill's position. Instantly Mr. Mill rose in reply, and now with a voice distinctly audible in every part of the House he pointed out the irrelevancy of Mr. Ayrton's arguments and reiterated his own with still greater force of illustration. As soon as Mr. Mill was seated, Mr. Lowe, whom John Bright the other day described as the " intellectual gladiator " of the House, advanced to the charge against the new member. Mr. Lowe was a foeman worthy of his steel; and again this scholarly recluse, with his intellectual eye as clear and penetrating in the crowded assemblage as it was wont to be in the voiceless company of his books, rose and met the onset of Mr. Lowe, covering the vital point of his own argument and thrusting his sword exactly through the middle of his antagonist's. When Mr. Mill took his seat every intelligent man felt that a new and, of its kind, an unsurpassed power had joined the House of Commons. His second and third speeches showed what the first could not,—that the great dialectic abilities of Mr. Mill are capable of being brought to bear in Parliament in hand-to-hand contests, in running debate, in logical repartee.

Passing over Mr. Mill's great argument on the reform bill, which I did not hear—an argument the depth and massiveness of which are daily growing in the appreciation of the country —I come to the memorable speech I have already referred to, delivered last Tuesday evening. The subject of discussion was again a bucolic one, the reduction of the duty on malt; and the resolution to that effect had been moved by Sir Fitzroy Kelly, the predestined lord chancellor of the next Tory ministry. The debate had dragged itself along over leagues of statistics and of platitudes. Not a ray of genuine thought, not a flash of enlivening sentiment, had been emitted, when, at last, Mr. Mill rose to second an amendment, the point of which was that any redundancy of revenue should be applied, not to a remission of the malt tax, but to a payment of the national debt. Not more than seventy members were then left in the house. Mr. Bright, Mr. Disraeli, Lord Stanley, had long since fled. On the treasury bench Mr. Gladstone was quite alone—

> "A pillar of state: deep on his front engraven,
> Deliberation sat and public care;
> With Atlantean shoulders fit to bear
> The weight of mightiest monarchies."

On the Tory side, the only eminent man left to Sir Fitzroy was Bulwer-Lytton, whose long, meagre, uncouth form had writhed and twisted impatiently upon his seat, and who, upon the appearance of Mr. Mill, bent far forward with his chin in his left hand and the elbow resting on his knee, while his eyes glared intently from beneath the shade of his broad-brimmed hat. On Mr. Mill's rising, two or three country members noisily stalked out of the room; a few members on the Liberal side moved still nearer to Mr. Mill; and all who remained sat in attitudes of respectful attention. I need not recapitulate the speech which he then made. His voice, though tremulous and by no means loud, was perfectly distinct, and every syllable from his lips was audible in every part of the House. His manner was the perfection of dignified, scholarly, and sincere speaking; almost pathetic in its earnest tones; not facile with the glibness of practised oratory, yet fluent with the deliberation of one who is master alike of deep thought and of fitting words. It is strange, the magic there is in the slightest touch of genius upon an assemblage, however weary, however dull. The first real statesmanly thought born to us during all the long hours of that night seemed to open the heavens above our heads, and to let in light and the atmosphere of life. All felt the witchery of the spell; and the climax of admiration and of excitement was reached when, at the close of his compact and unanswerable demonstration, he uttered that exquisite peroration which one old member of Parliament told me was the most poetical and eloquent passage heard there for many years:

"I beg very strongly indeed to press upon the House the duty of taking these things into serious consideration, in the name of that dutiful concern for posterity which has been very strong in every nation that ever did anything great, and which has never left the minds of any such nation until, as in the case of the Romans under the empire, it was already falling into decrepitude and ceasing to be a nation. . . . Whatever has been done for mankind by the idea of posterity—whatever has been done for mankind by philanthropic concern for posterity—by a conscientious sense of duty for posterity—even by the less pure but still noble ambition of being remembered and honored by them—all this we owe to posterity, and all this it is our duty, to the best of our limited ability, to repay. All the great deeds of the founders of nations, and of those second founders of nations, the great reformers—all that has been done for us by the authors of those laws and institutions to which free countries are indebted for their freedom, and well-governed countries for their good government—all the heroic lives which have been lived and the deaths which have been died in defence of liberty and law against despotism and tyranny, from Marathon and Salamis down to Leipsic and Waterloo—all those traditions of wisdom and of virtue which are enshrined in the history and literature of the past—all the schools and universities by which the culture of a former time has been brought down to us, and all that culture itself—all that we owe to the great masters of human thought, to the great masters of human emotion—all this is ours, because those who preceded us have taken thought for posterity."

Great as must be the delight of every one who only reads these sentences and the remainder of the passage from which they are torn, that delight cannot compare with our rapt astonishment who actually heard them; with our startled and breathless joy as in the moment of their conception they came dropping so timidly, with so sweet and gentle a cadence, with so unassuming a beauty, with a passionate earnestness so veiled and chained by intellectual refinement, from the quivering lips of the speaker. There was in his manner nothing of the triumphant complacency of mere rhetoric, nothing of the muscularity and physical jubilance of mere oratory. It was altogether and infinitely above it. It was pure, ethereal, unearthly. The immediate effect of that speech was indescribable; while upon the public, who have been reading it and discussing it ever since, its effect seems likely to be profound and lasting.

21 April, 1866.

THE NEW REFORM MOVEMENT

> " Hail, England of my children !—not this den
> Of vermin and their victims, nicknamed free—
> Isle of the Future !—will thy sons be men,
> Or Corn-Law bipeds ? Lo ! I turn to thee
> Not hopeless in my fear. . . .
> What will our children's sons in thee behold !
> Will souls be cheap that bodies may be sold !"
> —EBENEZER ELLIOTT, 1830.

AS the French Revolution was the historic corollary of the American Revolution, so the new reform bill in England, which now disgusts the Tories and fills all Liberal hearts with hope, is a distinct echo of the surrender of Lee. This latest programme for extending the liberties of Englishmen was written by the same iron pen which wrote that Americans, whether originally derived from Europe or from Africa, were not to be deprived of theirs.

There seems to be a mystic ocean of spiritual forces heaving its tides on all shores, more subtile than the atmosphere, more diffusive and penetrating than light, rising higher than the tops of those "mountains interposed" which "make enemies of nations"; and the wave which sprang upward twelve months ago, as Grant's victorious sword smote its waters, has rolled across the bosom of Christendom. It is hard to give an adequate picture of the terrible prostration of the Liberal cause in England between 1860 and 1865, in consequence of the prostration of the national cause in America. It was with a jubilant frenzy that the Tories contemplated the bursting of the bubble republic. Jeff. Davis and Stonewall Jackson were doing what the Tories had tried in vain to do: they were refuting the arguments of Cobden and Bright, and were unravelling that beautiful but dangerous tapestry of democratic success, whose radiant figures, woven by citizen hands, had proved all too bewitching to the people of the old world. "Talk no more of popularizing the government of England; you see what popular government comes to." With the exception of those rare men and women here who, in the dark days of our war, would not bate one jot of heart or hope—to whom was given

> " The instinct that can tell
>   That God is on the field, when He
>   Is most invisible "—

the mouths of English Liberals were smitten

dumb. The cause of the people lay in syncope. But when at last the armed Democracy of America, after so many blunders and so many humiliations, proved not only its incomparable capacity for war, but its incomparable capacity for peace,—its self-control, its political magnanimity, its new and splendid principle of loyalty and national unity,—then it was that in all civilized lands faith in government by the people awoke to a new life. Thus the capture of Richmond meant, among sundry other things, the revival in England of its old movement for enlarging the suffrage.

Just before Easter, Mr. Gladstone—perhaps the most variously gifted English statesman since Edmund Burke—brought in the government measure for enlarging the basis of representation. The House of Commons is composed of two kinds of members: those who represent counties, thence called knights of the shire; and those who represent towns or boroughs, thence called burgesses. Since the reform bill of 1832, the qualification for the county vote has been to live in a house worth $250 a year; and for the borough vote, to live in a house worth $50 a year. The essence of the new bill is a reduction of this qualification, in the former case to $70 and in the latter to $35, thereby increasing the number of voters in England and Wales by about four hundred thousand. The case of Scotland and Ireland, where the conditions of voting are different, was left for future consideration. To judge more intelligently of the bearings of the new bill, it is necessary to remember that the adult male population of England and Wales is five and a half millions; that of this number only nine hundred thousand already possess votes; and that, if Mr. Gladstone's measure shall be adopted, the number of Englishmen who can exercise this simple right of citizenship in their native land will still be only thirteen hundred thousand, or about one fourth of the whole male population of voting age.

At first glance it might seem to an American that so slight a concession to the vast unrepresented class of Britons would be scarcely worth the trouble of any great party to propose, much less of any great party to resist; and that, if the measure fell, it would do so in consequence of Parliament going to sleep over a proposition which had not enough in it to keep anybody awake. Moreover, it might be expected that the mass of Englishmen would receive such a recognition of their existence with a mixture of indignation and contempt, spurning it as a crumb from the rich men's tables, too paltry even to be picked up from the floor. Yet, on the one hand, the people have welcomed the proffered boon with grateful enthusiasm; while on the other, the obstructives have been for several weeks in a state of political fever-and-ague—now flushed with wrath, now shivering with alarm—at the bare thought of this hideous overture to radicalism and democracy. And both are right. The people have reason for their gladness, the obstructives for their fury and fright. The former perceive that, while the number of voters to be added is small in proportion to the whole population of the country, it is not small in proportion to those who at present possess votes; and that, if four hundred thousand of their friends now get inside the pale of the constitution, they will speedily make room for four hundred thousand more. The obstructives possess instinct even where they do not seem to possess reason; and the selfishness of hereditary privilege is gifted with infallibility upon just one subject—the approach of danger to itself:

> "By the pricking of my thumbs
> Something wicked this way comes."

Hitherto the legislation of this country has been by the privileged few in the interests of themselves. An acre of land has wielded more influence than a square mile of humanity. Houses have been infinitely more precious than hearts and brains. For many ages this sort of thing having been going on; the soil having dictated laws to those who tilled it; the houses having regulated the rights of those who lived in them; the men born to do no work having arranged the obligations of the men born to do all the work; what more inevitable than that the result should be a vast fabric of selfish laws—such as those for acquiring land, entailing property, preserving game, coercing tenants, regulating labor, and supporting an opulent hierarchy; and just as the first reform bill shook this huge fabric of selfishness, and removed some of its most outrageous features, the present reform bill will continue the process to precisely the extent to which it enables the people to get a hand in selecting their own lawmakers.

At this writing, the fate of Mr. Gladstone's measure cannot be foretold. The bill has indeed passed its second reading, but by the miserable majority of five out of a house of six hundred and thirty-one; and it may be doubted whether now it will not be picked to pieces and annihilated in committee.

The debates upon the measure have continued, with many interruptions, over a period of six weeks, and have brought out on both sides powers of reasoning, criticism, wit, sarcasm, invective, and lofty eloquence, worthy of the illustrious assemblage in which they were displayed—reviving the echo of those impassioned and memorable orations in 1831-2, on the same great theme, when the house rang with the powerful and fervid appeals of Lord John Russell and the sonorous periods of the youthful Macaulay. On the side of the Opposition there have been three speeches which tower above the rest—those of Mr. Disraeli, Lord Stanley, and Mr. Robert Lowe; while, on the side of the government, a similar pre-eminence attaches to the efforts of John Stuart Mill, Mr. Coleridge, John Bright, and Mr. Gladstone.

I said the fate of this bill is yet doubtful. But one thing is not doubtful: if this moderate measure is defeated, and the government is driven from office, the people of England will take up the cause of their champions with a fierce and resolute energy that will be satisfied only by a measure far more sweeping and comprehensive. Last Saturday morning, just as the gray dawn was about breaking over the towers of Westminster Palace, Mr. Gladstone, the affluent, the peerless statesman, than whom no knight of King Arthur's best ever fought with a more chivalrous valor, concluded a magnificent oration with these noble words:

" But, sir, we are assailed : this bill is in a state of crisis and of peril, and the government along with it. We stand or fall with it, as has been declared by my noble friend. We stand with it now ; we may fall with it a short time hence ; and, if we do, we shall rise with it hereafter. I shall not attempt to measure with precision the forces that are to be arrayed in the coming struggle. Perhaps the great division of to-night is not the last that must take place in the struggle. You may possibly succeed at some point of the contest. You may drive us from our seats. You may bury the bill that we have introduced ; but for its epitaph we will write upon its gravestone this line, with certain confidence in its fulfilment :

' Exoriare aliquis nostris ex ossibus ultor.'

You cannot fight against the future. Time is on our side. The great social forces which move on in their might and majesty, and which the tumult of our debates does not for a moment impede or disturb—those great social forces are against you ; they are marshalled on our side, and the banner which we now carry, though perhaps at some moment it may droop over our sinking heads, yet it soon again will float in the eye of heaven ; and it will be borne by the firm hands of the united people of the three kingdoms, perhaps not to an easy, but to a certain and to a not distant, victory."

30 April, 1866.

MR. GLADSTONE IN DEFEAT

IN Harriet Martineau's "History of the Peace" we have a graphic description of the fierce parliamentary contests of 1827, of George Canning, the great parliamentary leader of that period, and of the foes who hated him and hounded him to death; and it has seemed to me that her words for that occasion would form an almost perfect picture of the stormy parliamentary session that is at this moment drawing toward a close, and of the great parliamentary leader whose transcendent abilities have this year been unveiled against a hostility as malignant, as subtle, and as persistent, as his great master was encountering thirty-nine years ago:

"The session had lasted two months after the reassembling of Parliament on the first of May. It was a season of turbulence and rancor, which it is painful and humbling to look back upon. The minister was the professed object of the rancor, and it was he who sank under it; but not even he, with all his powers, and all his attributes of offence, could have caused such perturbation at another time and in another position. Those who had differed from his former politics, and those who detested his present aims; all who had suffered under his sarcastic wit; all who were disappointed that he had overcome his late difficulties; all who were jealous of a political adventurer having risen over the heads of the aristocracies both of birth and of political administration, stimulated one another to insult, and to overpower, if they could, the minister who stood exposed to all attacks, incapable of aid because himself so immeasurably greater than all who would have aided, as than all who attacked him. It is universally agreed that personality and insult were never before so rank in any assembly of English gentlemen as now, during the two months following Mr. Canning's accession to the premiership."

When the present Parliament opened in February, it was under a new leader. The brave and merry old man, who, by personal prestige, by unerring tact, by tingling jest, and by an occasional outburst of admirable bullying, had for almost a generation swayed the House at his will, was never more to be seen on the treasury bench, slumbering beneath his hat-brim. Mr. Gladstone sat there his nominal successor; it remained to be shown whether he was his actual successor. And the real significance of this extraordinary, this historical session, is wrapped in that problem. Through all wranglings about the cattle plague, about Jamaica, about reform bills, the interior and the essential trial has been of Mr. Gladstone's metal for leadership—of his presence of mind, self-command, pluck, grit, physical endurance, and intellectual versatility.

During the first few weeks of the session, business moved on smoothly enough. His enemies on the opposite side, his enemies on his own side, held back, scabbarded their swords, watched him with sleepless eye and ear. Now and then, even before the Easter recess, some champion would sally forth and engage his prowess; but it was not until after the brief holiday that a general onslaught was made. Alarmed at the amazing ascendancy that Mr. Gladstone was acquiring over the nation, and at the display of those marvellous qualities which had almost justified Mr. Mill's verdict that Gladstone is " the greatest parliamentary leader of the present century, and perhaps since the Stuarts," they commenced their aggressive movement; they assailed him simultaneously from every quarter, with every kind of weapon, with every mode of attack. The history of the last six weeks is the history of a deliberate and desperate personal dead-set against the man they envied, hated, feared. Beneath all their denunciations of the reform bill ran the undertone of personal hostility to the statesman who had proposed it; and in the boisterous shouts which went up a week ago from Tory squires and treacherous Liberals over the defeat of the government—shouts rising louder and louder, and renewed again and again with a sort of insanity of joy—there was distinctly audible the harsh note of ungenerous glee over what "The Saturday Review" is pleased to describe as "the collapse of a great man."

The prospects of the liberal cause in England—the issues of those momentous designs of a statesmanship more enlightened and magnanimous than Europe has hitherto seen—are seemingly so bound up with the political future of Mr. Gladstone, that it will repay us to glance at the causes of this relentless personal opposition.

1. There is one phrase which, in the upper circles of English society, is more damning to the man to whom it may be applied than almost any other in the whole vocabulary of depreciation. It is the phrase " political adventurer," the modern synonym of "novus homo"— the phrase with which the Roman patricians sought to blast the career of Cicero; the phrase which, in our own century, has been hurled by English patricians at the greatest statesmen in it—at Canning, Huskisson,

Henry Brougham, Macaulay, Richard Cobden, and William Ewart Gladstone. The unpardonable offence of Mr. Gladstone is that he neither got himself born nor got himself married into any of the thirty-one great governing families of England. It is true that he is wealthy, that his father was a baronet, that the associations of his life have been aristocratic; yet he is neither a Cavendish, nor a Courtney, nor a Stanley, nor a Cecil. By his genius, by his goodness, by his past renown, by his stupendous popularity, they perceive that Mr. Gladstone is to be England's real monarch for the next decade and a half. They are wrathful that another supreme minister has risen from the middle class. Either Mr. Gladstone should not have been so great a man, or he should not have allowed himself to be born out of their set.

2. The second reason to explain the opposition to him is one even more ignoble—the envy of old comrades at his success. By the trophy of this Miltiades there are some scores of ambitious fellows in Parliament who cannot sleep. The men who witnessed the glory of Lord Palmerston's later years could exult in it with a satisfaction unalloyed by so base a passion as I now refer to: he was of an elder generation, and was above the range of their jealousy. But such illustrious personages as Mr. Robert Lowe,

Mr. Laing, Mr. Horsman, Sir Robert Peel, Lord Cranbourne, Lord A. Montagu, are said to look upon themselves as the equals of Mr. Gladstone, because they are his contemporaries; and they seem unable to forgive him for the fact that the general opinion of England does not exactly coincide with their own in that respect.

3. There is one other serious objection to Mr. Gladstone, operating not alone upon those to whom I have already referred, but upon a multitude of others: he is a dead-in-earnest man. His political views are not jests, but convictions. With him political life seems to be neither an ostentation, nor a disguised selfishness, nor a comedy, but a consecration. The principal English politicians, however, who are just now at the surface, have grown up under the example of Lord Palmerston, and have been morally debauched by the success of that splendid political Sadducee. With a facile smile, a jovial bearing, incredulous as to the higher maxims of public conduct, worldly, materialistic, they look upon statesmanship as a highly respectable and remunerative farce; they regard election pledges as a play with words; they admire the gift of badinage as the chief attribute of a first minister; and they think the most serious plea sufficiently refuted by the most trivial pun. Of course, such men

cannot comprehend earnestness : it arouses either their ridicule or their rage. When they see it in ordinary men, they laugh at it; they banter it; they try to smother it beneath a shower of

"Quips and cranks and wanton wiles."

But when they behold this spirit in the alliance of personal greatness, kindling an eloquence whose majesty overwhelms them, vitalizing a scholarship whose vastness fills them with awe, crowning and glorifying a nature whose dignity silences the patter of their shallow facetiousness, what is left to them but hate—a hostility hardened into utter vindictiveness, and gnashing its teeth in an ecstasy of loathing ?

No discerning person could have sat in the House of Commons this session, could have heard the tone of the opposing speeches, could have seen and heard how " the first assembly of gentlemen in the world " was capable of resolving itself into a zoölogical garden of wild beasts, of magpies and monkeys, howling, bellowing, screeching, chattering, in one prolonged chorus of brutal fury against the Chancellor of the Exchequer, without perceiving that there was an antagonism between him and them only to be explained by that tremendous gulf of moral unlikeness of which I have spoken.

But the agony is now over. England is to have a Tory government. It may last a few weeks; it may last a few months; but not long will the people endure it. Probably before the first anniversary of his resignation the heart of England will call again to the foremost place her best-beloved and her ablest statesman.

On the whole, the interregnum is not to be regretted. It will be good for England to test by responsibility the new methods of Conservatism. It will be good for the Liberal party to have an experience of adversity. It will be pre-eminently good for Mr. Gladstone to have a year of repose.

This very evening I went down to the House to hear the ministerial statement of the Queen's decision. I found New Palace Yard thronged with people eager to see the arrival of the chieftains of both parties, and before entering the House I waited to witness the sort of reception which the several leaders would get from that fearless and tumultuous parliament out-of-doors. An English crowd never minces matters, or expresses itself with ambiguity. On this occasion they growled, and groaned, and shook their fists at the men who have defeated the measure for the people's enfranchisement; and, as they recognized the champions of the people's cause, they heaped cheers and benedictions upon their heads. But just as Big Ben sounded from his regal tower the hour of six, we heard a roar of voices far away down Parliament Street, and presently Mr. Gladstone, with Mrs. Gladstone at his side, drove in an open carriage into the yard. How the hats went off from those tossing heads, how the cheers went up from those palpitating throats! Had he been king, he could not have had a kinglier reception. Climbing upon one of the pilasters of Westminster Hall, holding on with one hand, swinging my hat with the other, and mingling my not very despicable trans-atlantic shouts with that immense gush of British enthusiasm, I had a fine view of the minister who was just to announce that the Queen had accepted his resignation. He has the face and the port of a statesman. He lifted his hat and responded to the salutes of the people, but he looked pale, and haggard, and weary. As the carriage swept round under the archway leading to the members' private entrance, Mrs. Gladstone rose, and threw back over the multitudes a look of inexpressible happiness, and gratitude, and wifely pride. How welcome to the jaded statesman must be this release from the toils of office! And this interlude of much-needed rest may save him from the fate of so many of his predecessors, and may preserve to England a life which has already given a new lustre to English eloquence and to English statesmanship, and a new impulse to the enlightenment and happiness of mankind.

26 June, 1866.

THE ACCUSATION AGAINST MR. GLADSTONE

A GIFTED American woman the other day had a seat in that dark, grated, oriental cage at the northern end of the House of Commons, which the finest gentlemen in England set apart for the use and obscuration of their fair visitors. After spending some hours in studying the faces of the political and literary celebrities congregated far below her, she replied to my demand for her verdict by uttering about the best parliamentary criticism I remember to have heard: "They all look so extremely fond of their dinners—except—except —Mr. Gladstone." I could not help rejoining, "So much the worse for Mr. Gladstone."

In passing the eye over those crowded benches of robust senators, of ruddy, loud-lunged and abdominous patriots—heroic defenders of church, state, and dinner-hour—faithful representatives, if not of the political aspirations, at least of the gastronomic energies of Britain; and then, in resting the gaze upon the most interesting personage in the House, upon Mr. Gladstone's tall, finely proportioned, yet slender frame, upon his pale, intellectual, sensitive face, it is impossible not to feel a momentary regret that he has not more of the roast-beef-and-plum-pudding look, that he has not something of the adipose massiveness, something of the coarseness of physical texture, by which to meet the onsets of so much coarseness and massiveness about him. "A small infusion of the alderman," says Dean Swift, "is necessary to those who are employed in public affairs." Mr. Gladstone's organization seems too fine, too delicate and nervous, in a word, too noble, for his antagonists. One feels that their outward walls of brawn and blubber may protect them from the diamond-point of his spear, even as General Jackson's cotton-bales absorbed the bullets of the enemy at New Orleans; and we would almost be willing to lose a portion of the exquisite quality of Mr. Gladstone's eloquence, if by an addition of some callosity of fibre he could be spared the pain to which we fear his fineness of nature subjects him. Byron once told Lady Blessington that "he hoped his daughter had not poetical genius," as the price paid for its advantages was too high. Mr. Gladstone has the temperament both of a poet and of a scholar; and it seems a sort of desecration that it be exposed to the rough antagonism of bellowing squires and fox-hunters. Yet we may also remember that only he who can suffer deeply can enjoy deeply; and that while the beauty and exquisiteness of Mr. Gladstone's organization makes him the victim of taunts that would rebound from the crass cuticle of some other men, doubtless he has consolations which only such souls as he can know—the refreshment of lofty and therefore harmonizing thought, the rapture of noble emotion, the prevision of ultimate victory, and what Sir Philip Sidney calls " the strong appetites of honor."

My last letter was about Mr. Gladstone; and, as at the end of it I was very far from the woe which Voltaire pronounced upon " the man who says all he has to say upon any subject," this letter shall be about Mr. Gladstone also. A very serious accusation is being pressed against him. All the Tory papers and all the toryized Whig ones are ringing the changes upon Mr. Gladstone's " haughty bearing " in the house, upon his " imperious spirit," and especially upon the alleged " irascibility of his temper "; and they constantly affirm that the catastrophe to his reform bill and to his administration was largely owing to his display of these qualities. I am sorry to observe the repetition of this cruel and absolutely false accusation in certain American papers. For example, the able and usually just London correspondent

of the " New York Times " makes this remark:
" Mr. Gladstone has not distinguished himself
as a leader. He is irritable, petulant, wavering,
and dictatorial." That statement, made I
venture to suggest from hearsay rather than
from actual observation this session, is a splendid example of the perfect antithesis of the
truth.

The fame of Mr. Gladstone is a sacred gift
to the world, and something of which every
lover of human progress has a right to be jealous. This accusation, uttered in England, can
be easily refuted in England; but when it is
conveyed to another hemisphere, where eye-
and ear-witnesses of Mr. Gladstone's recent
career are not at hand to deal with it, the misrepresentation is in danger of being long-lived.

" Mr. Gladstone has not distinguished himself as a leader!" Well, the writer of this
statement has opposed to him the tolerably
valuable opinion of John Stuart Mill, whose
estimate of Mr. Gladstone as a leader places
him above Palmerston, above Sir Robert Peel,
above Canning, above the younger Pitt, and,
with a qualification, even above the elder Pitt
and Sir Robert Walpole. In truth, Mr. Gladstone's bearing since he became leader has been
so magnificent, both in the House and out of
it, that he has drawn to himself the great Liberal party by an enthusiasm almost unequalled

in the history of England; he has extorted the loud and earnest all-hail of the greatest intellects in the kingdom; and he has contrived to make his name the symbol of the people's hopes and the battle-cry that rouses like the sound of a bugle. At this moment the air of these islands is filled with the watchword, " Gladstone and Reform." If all this be failure, it would be interesting to know what is success.

As to his having been lacking in command of his temper, and in proper deference to the House, since he became its leader, I believe that a statement more baseless it would be impossible to manufacture. The question becomes a very simple one of testimony. I will not invite myself into the witness-box, although I could testify that, whenever I have enjoyed the privilege of being in the House of Commons, I have been struck with admiration at the dignified and graceful courtesy of Mr. Gladstone; at the charm and fascination of his bearing; at the total absence of any tinge of arrogance in his treatment of other members; at his unflagging attention to every reasonable appeal, from whatever quarter of the room; at his forbearance toward foes who were raging for his destruction; at his marvellous patience under insults the most annoying and unseemly. I will summon to the stand two witnesses of the highest eminence and of the most unquestionable reliability.

In a speech at Lambeth, on the 22d of June, Mr. Thomas Hughes—our " Tom Brown " of the " School Days "—made these remarks:

" Then it is said that the Liberal majority has been lost through Mr. Gladstone's imperiousness. I ask you to look this matter fairly in the face. Is it a proof of imperiousness that Mr. Gladstone has given up to the opposition every point except those which he deemed absolutely material? Is that the conduct of a haughty and intolerant man, who tries to put down honest opposition? Never was there a baser calumny uttered against a great man. My admiration for that noble man has been growing all through the session, when I saw how earnestly he battled to keep the promises he had made. Give me the leader who acts as if he had a work to accomplish, as if a woe was on him if he did not accomplish it. It is a disgrace to the House of Commons that they don't know a great man when they see him. All this session they have been like a pack of hounds let loose on the leader of the House of Commons."

The highly respected member for the city of Cork, Mr. John Francis Maguire, who must be known in America by his admirable " Biography of Father Mathew," has just made public a letter, from which I take the following sentences:

"And how did the people's champion bear himself in this protracted struggle? I watched him with singular interest in all the varying fortunes of the campaign—for that it was; and I must conscientiously admit that I do not believe that any statesman, having a due regard to his own honor, could have borne himself with more loyalty to his cause, or with a juster deference to the legitimate wishes of the House. From his very organization he must be specially susceptible to taunt, sneer, insinuation, however delicate or covert it may be; and Heaven knows these were rained on his head for four long months; yet I do not remember a single instance in which he lost his temper, compromised his dignity, or transgressed the limits of that decorum which is looked for in a minister of the crown, human as he must be. He was necessarily compelled at times to employ the same weapons that were directed against him; but he has on many occasions held back his hand rather than strike, though the enemy's armor was all agape with rents and crevices, or though his opponent was naked to the thrust. I shall say nothing of his marvellous endurance, as night after night he was faithfully at his post, ever on the alert, ready at any moment to meet his opponents, whatever their mode or manner of attack; or how, when the emergency called for a fuller display of his powers and a bolder enunciation of the living and essential principles of his measures, his oratory borrowed majesty from the imminence of the peril, and his words swelled like the deep notes of an organ, or startled like the blast of a trumpet. Let me only say that he fell with honor—fell, but to rise stronger than ever in the public conviction of his honesty and truth."

Socrates, on one occasion, being complimented for having the best possible temper in the world, replied that he had " the worst possible temper with the best possible control of it." I do not say that the former part of this Socratic confession would exactly apply to Mr. Gladstone, but he has shown that the latter part would do so. A finely strung, excitable, sensitive man, he has, in several emergencies, while still in a subordinate position, grown extremely angry in the House of Commons; he has got into a passion; and, giving the rein to his boundless powers of sarcasm and invective, he has scourged his antagonists to his own and their content. Upon the death of Lord Palmerston, almost the only doubt in the minds of Mr. Gladstone's admirers was whether he could always and infallibly command that high and stormy spirit of his; for it would be fatal to a leader of the House if his opponents knew that, by a series of judiciously contrived insults, they could throw him off his guard. The Tories of all shades and grades raised the cry that he would certainly lose his temper; and they evidently resolved that their prediction should come true. They worried him, tormented him, insidiously attacked him; and they have been exceedingly angry because they could not make him so. When one of their champion brow-beaters, like Mr. Lowe, of rare vituperative genius, has risen to conduct an attack, a scene like this has been usually presented : Mr. Gladstone would quietly settle far down on the treasury bench, stretch out his legs in front of him, and there, with his feet against the base of the table, his hands folded over his breast, the back of his head against the back of the bench, his pale, sad, but resolute face upturned, his eyes closed or gazing at the lighted roof of the chamber, he would receive the peltings of the storm; and hour after hour, as the assaults raved on, he would make no sign of passion or resentment, nor any movement, save occasionally when some taunt of peculiar malignity would seem to send a pang to his heart and a nervous twitching for an instant across his face.

Wise, affluent, and magnanimous statesman! Hitherto renowned for strength to do, and henceforth worthy of the grander renown of strength to suffer! Mightier from defeat than your enemies are from victory, advancing in the impenetrable armor of integrity, sustained by the benedictions of Heaven, and cheered by the homage and love of the millions who in all quarters of the globe speak the mother-speech of England, may your power be as great as your beneficent purpose, and may your stately career long continue to shed gladness on palace and on cottage, to lighten the burdens of the weary, to uplift those whom cruel circumstance has depressed, and to leave to the generations of mankind a model of the highest Christian statesmanship!

4 July, 1866.

THE HOUSE OF COMMONS

I

ITS LOCAL HABITATION

THAT is an era in a man's life—especially in an American's life—the day on which he first sees this imperial assemblage, the oldest, the wealthiest, the most cultivated, and the most powerful legislative body in the world —the parent and prototype of our own House of Representatives.

It was under very fortunate circumstances that, a little more than three years ago, I got my first glimpse of "that dense, troubled body," as Boswell calls it. A member of the House, who happened also to be a member of Lord Palmerston's government, very kindly invited me to accompany him thither; and on our way, and after our arrival, he gave me just the information which a stranger needed to possess, and which would have been very impressive even upon a nature not particularly sensitive to the grandeur of thronging and venerable historical associations.

We started from one of the offices in Whitehall, and passed beneath the window through which Charles I. was lifted out to his execution; we cast a look into Downing Street—narrow, close, and dark—but for so many generations the official residence of the prime minister of England; on one side we saw Whitehall Gardens, where the great Sir Robert Peel used to live in wealth and splendor, and on the other side King Street, where a greater than he, the author of "The Faery Queen," "died for lack of bread"; as we reached the bottom of Parliament Street there rose full before us the majestic Abbey, where the monarchs of England are crowned, and where, after a mightier monarch has discrowned them, they repose from the splendors of royalty; then passing beneath a statue of Canning, and catching a view of an obscure court, on which are written in homely and prosaic letters those thrilling words, "Poets' Corner," we came into New Palace Yard, which Macaulay has described as being full of all manner of illustrious people—royal and noble beauties, princes, peers, poets, scholars, historians, and wits—early on the morning of the day on which Sheridan delivered his splendid pinchbeck philippic against Warren Hastings. From this yard is the main entrance to old Westminster Hall, which now serves as an immense vestibule for the law courts and for the Houses of Parliament, and which by a beautiful, even if undesigned, propriety is kept absolutely empty of all decorations, and even of ordinary furniture, that it may be occupied wholly by the centuries of reminiscences—vast, tragic, heroic, superb, or pitiful—which fill it forever with their invisible populations. As I heard the echoes of our own feet upon the stony floor, and gazed up at the lofty arches of the roof, it was only difficult to keep within decorous bounds the tide of emotion so natural to one from over the sea who stands in Westminster Hall for the first time; and it required no effort of the imagination for me to re-enact the tremendous scenes which have taken place here; to see in the great room the continuous march of that mighty procession of renowned men and women who have spoken, laughed, and wept here; to see the haughty form of William Rufus, as he surveys " the forced levies of unhappy Saxon workmen " who laid the foundations of this Hall, and reared with an unrequited agony of toil its stately walls, and to hear the harsh voice of the tyrant as he boasts that this should be only as a bed-chamber compared with the magnificence of the pile which he intended to erect by its side; to see Richard II. keeping a merry Christmas here in 1397, and entertaining ten thousand guests at his table, and then the stormy Parliament meeting here and deposing him from his throne in favor of Harry of Bolingbroke; to see pacing up and down these stones the greatest kings, soldiers, judges, and statesmen whom England ever had; to see the inauguration of Cromwell as Lord Protector, and, at the restoration, his head upon a pole between the skulls of Ireton and Bradshaw; to see the trials of William Wallace and Sir Thomas More, of the Protector Somerset, and Stafford, and Charles I., and Lord Russell, and Algernon Sidney; to hear the cheers which within these walls greeted the acquittal of the seven bishops under James II.; and, nobler still, to hear the indignant voices of Fox, Burke, and Sheridan roused to their loftiest eloquence by the crimes of Hastings, and by the sufferings of those millions in India who had no voice nor language to tell their wrongs.

Leaving this consecrated room, we had to pass through various halls and corridors before we got to the Chamber of the Commons: first, St. Stephen's Hall, whose sides are lined by statues of twelve famous commoners—Falkland, Hampden, Clarendon, Selden, Walpole, Somers, Mansfield, Chatham, Pitt, Fox, Burke, and Grattan; then the great central octagon hall; then a long corridor, on whose walls are frescos representing memorable scenes in English history; and, finally, a smaller octagon hall, opening into the room of the great legislature itself.

Since the interest which an American feels in the House of Commons belongs much more to the past than to the present, being chiefly derived from his recollection of the great deeds which have been achieved by it for constitutional freedom, and of the great men who in former ages have been distinguished in it for their genius, their courage, and their love of liberty, it seems only a fitting preparation that his entrance from the bustling realism of London thoroughfares should be not too immediate and too abrupt; but that, passing along these ancient streets of Westminster, whose very names are eloquent with historic story, and through these halls and courts, where kings have banqueted, where warriors have trod, where martyrs have borne high testimony, and amid these noble columns and statues, which speak to him of heroic ages and heroic men, alike departed and immortal, his eyes should first be purged of the dust of modern and vulgar things by the euphrasy of antique suggestion, and his spirit lifted to a proper historical enthusiasm.

The physical appointments of the Commons Chamber are easily given. It is a room—rich, massy, sombre—sixty-nine feet long, forty-five feet wide, forty-four feet high, with windows of stained glass, walls of carved oak, and ceiling covered with ornamentation. The Speaker's chair, which is a sort of canopied and cushioned recess, stands at the northern end; and immediately in front is the desk for the clerk and his two assistants; and still in front of that, and protruding far into the great dividing aisle which runs the whole length of the room, is the table of the House. Upon this table, bills, petitions, and other documents are laid. If a member wishes to use pen and ink, he leaves his seat and goes to this table for the purpose; at this table ministers stand to make their statements, laying upon it their dispatch-boxes, spreading out over it their memoranda, often using it as a rest for their elbows as they lazily meander through their speeches; and across this table the chiefs of the hostile parties grin, scowl, and gesticulate at each other, and hurl fact, argument, sarcasm, or defiance, as the case requires. The seats provided for members are not chairs, as in our Congress, but long, leather-covered benches; which, instead of being ranged crosswise in the room to face the Speaker, extend lengthwise along the sides, leaving the broad aisle in the middle.

By common consent, and from the earliest times, members have taken their seats in the House according to their party alliances and proclivities. The front bench on the right of the Speaker is called the treasury bench, and is always occupied by the Chancellor of the Exchequer, who is generally the leader of the House, and by such other members of the government as are commoners. The immediate adherents of the party in power take the benches just behind; while the allegiance of other members to the reigning party is indicated on a scale of gradually lessening attachment in proportion as their seats recede from the neighborhood of official greatness. On the other hand, the benches on the opposite side of the room—that is, to the left of the Speaker—are always occupied by the party out of office, and on a principle of arrangement analogous to that just described for the government side; the chief members of the opposition taking the front bench, and the rank and file covering the places in the rear. Distant readers of parliamentary doings are often puzzled by a term in frequent use—the gangway. For example, John Bright and John Stuart Mill, and their friends, are often referred to in the speeches as " the gentlemen below the gangway." This mysterious phrase merely denotes a narrow aisle on each side of the House, at right angles to the broad central aisle, and cutting the long rows of benches into two equal parts; and those sitting below this gangway, on either side of the House, are known as "independent members"—that is, as professing a general agreement with the party on the side they select, with a large reservation of privilege as to their action on special questions. Thus, John Bright has for many years occupied the upper end of the second bench below the gangway on whichever side of the House the Liberal party has sat; and Mr. Mill, last February, took the seat just behind Mr. Bright—that is, at the top of the third bench below the gangway. Of course, when there is a change of ministry, there is a change of places in the House; the party lately in opposition crossing over and taking exactly the places just vacated by the party lately in office.

It will be understood that this description merely applies to the floor of the House. There are galleries all round the room. Just above the Speaker's chair is the Reporters' gallery; and far above that, close to the very roof, is the miserable dark Mohammedan cage in which representatives of the dangerous sex are penned. Looking to the opposite end of the room, you would see a series of three galleries, called the Peers', the Speaker's, and the Strangers'—all small, and the last utterly inadequate to the desires and claims of those for whom it was intended.

I cannot say that the House of Commons in

its ordinary moods has ever seemed to me an inspiring spectacle. There are some men in it whom it is a delight to look upon and listen to. There is an abundance of culture in it, and high birth, and high breeding. There are, indeed, in it great scholars, great authors, great jurists, great wits, and some of the most perfect gentlemen in the world. But, as a whole, it is a spectacle which chills, darkens, and depresses. The House of Commons seems to me the crystallization of all that is least noble in the privileged classes of England—their selfishness, their arrogance, their greed of prerogative, their ambition for power, the indifferentism and the moral cowardice of their club-life, their misconception of the rights of the ignorant and the poor. The physical atmosphere of the House is detestable; its moral atmosphere is worse. The one gives headache, the other heartache. I confess that I can never look at those rows of well-fed fox-hunters and billiard-players, lordlings and parvenus, without Thomas Carlyle's words rising to my thoughts:

"Are they not there by trade, mission, and express appointment of themselves and others, to speak for the good of the British nation? Whatsoever great British interest can the least speak for itself, for that beyond all they are called to speak. They are either speakers for that great dumb toiling class which cannot speak, or they are nothing that one can well specify. 'Alas! the remote observer knows not the nature of parliaments; how parliaments extant there for the British nation's good find that they are extant withal for their own sake : how in Parliament there may chance to be a strong man, an original, clear-sighted, great-hearted, patient, and valiant man, or to be none such."

24 July, 1866.

THE HOUSE OF COMMONS

II

ITS PERSONAL COMPOSITION

IT is the nature of aristocracies to be absorbingly selfish; and a glaring political grievance of which Englishmen complain is only another illustration of the fact. While the aristocracy of England has by hereditary privilege the undisputed possession of one entire branch of the legislature, it also seeks to clutch as large a portion of the other branch as by its enormous wealth, its social prestige, and its ancient connections it is able to obtain. The Lower House is nominally a representation of the common people; but it is only since the great reform of 1832 that the middle or trading classes have had any appreciable voice in the selection of those who sit in the Commons House. Meanwhile, the outrageous case remains that the vast mass of the population below the traders—the sturdy millions who bear the industrial burdens of these islands—are political aliens in the land of their birth. After all the strenuous reform labors of a third of a century, after the incessant discussion of elemental politics, and the resolute agitation of popular rights for this long period, the latest general election has resulted in a House of Commons a very large portion of whose members are of patrician alliance, or would like to be, and are thus largely under the sway of the patrician class. By a careful analysis it appears that ninety-two members of the House of Commons, or about one seventh of the entire body, are sons, brothers, uncles, nephews, sons-in-law, or brothers-in-law of the thirty-one great governing families in England. Besides these, are members bearing the same relationships to the great Scotch and Irish families. In all there are about three hundred members of the great land-owning aristocracy of the country, besides country squires. There are one hundred and four naval or military officers, ninety-five barristers, ninety-three Cambridge men, and one hundred and twenty-seven Oxford men. Slightly under one hundred members appear ostensibly as merchants, manufacturers, bankers, brewers, or ship-owners; one hundred and twenty members are more or less concerned in the management of railways; whilst one hundred and fifteen are directors of insurance, banking, discount, and financial joint-stock companies, and one hundred and four are directors of miscellaneous companies.

Any one who would have a just idea of the course of English legislation, and of those interesting and momentous phases through which English politics are now passing, must bear in mind the broad fact to which I have called attention. It will not do to be deceived by names. The House of Commons is not a House of the common people. It is a House of territorial, professional, and commercial magnates, with a few philanthropists, many scholars, and more snobs. It is the stronghold, not of the English people, but of those great landed and moneyed classes that are still able to control the English people. Until a recent date, a considerable property qualification was necessary to render a citizen eligible for membership of this body; and it is still practically the rule that only men of fortune can aspire to the great honor of writing M.P. after their names. Parliamentary service brings no salary, but instead of that, the privilege of a more conspicuous social position and of heavier bills for current expenses; while the mere cost of getting elected to this luxury averages the pleasant little sum of $15,000 for each member. It was with some truth, therefore, that Edmond Beales, at the vast reform meeting at the Agricultural Hall, the other night, told John Stuart Mill and Peter Taylor that they belonged to a House whose very name was a mockery and a fraud.

Whatever there may be in the action of the House of Commons that is one-sided, distrustful, and timid; whatever that is reluctant in its recognition of popular claims; whatever in its consideration of depressed races that is overbearing and cold; whatever in its treatment of other nations—especially our own—that may have been inconsiderate and ungenerous, is to be taken, not as the thought or deed of England, but of what Mr. Disraeli loves to describe as " a great political order " in England.

Remembering the composition of this legislative body, who can be surprised at the essential character of class-legislation which marks its proceedings? It has all the strength and the weakness — the qualms, prejudices, and facilities—of the privileged minority. If you can imagine a question with which neither the interests nor the superstitions of that minority are implicated, you can imagine one on which the House will legislate with great wisdom, justice, and generosity; but be assured that, in the attention it may give to the pleas or the demands of the people, the lid never droops over the eye that is set to watch for the remotest chance of danger to itself. It is doubtful if John Bright even, with all his genius for stinging the grandee-class, ever made them more furious than he did last winter, when he said that the House of Commons was never in earnest about anything for the good of the people, and that only by clamor and intimidation was it ever brought to yield one popular concession. And, when these things are considered, what American can wonder at the preponderance of its sympathies with the oligarchs of the recent Confederacy, or fail to distinguish between the English aristocrats, who in our struggle were naturally against us, and the English common people, who were naturally with us?

By this study of the personal composition of the House of Commons we are enabled to estimate, not only the spirit of its legislation, but that strange code of courtesy which prevails within its walls. Parliamentary politeness is a very unique affair; and few natives or foreigners have reflected upon the subject deeply enough to account for its eccentricities and its contradictions. You are ushered into the gallery of a legislative chamber, where you have always understood are assembled the most scholarly and polished gentlemen of a highly civilized nation; and you see, adown the sombre hall, crowding the long files of benches, an array of black-coated statesmen, all sitting with their hats on. Not all; for here and there is an exception. Mr. Mill, for instance, with his sharp face and bald head, is a particularly shining exception. The active brain of Mr. Disraeli, too, seems to abhor the vacuum of his beaver; and Mr. Gladstone, also, is generally bare-headed. But it becomes obvious to you that the majority of the members are blessed with crania sufficiently dense to endure, within doors, the burden of their heavy hats for hours together. The first impression upon you is unpleasant. Your American chivalry starts at the incivility of forgetting that there are ladies in the room, even though you know that they are ladies caged. You wonder if " meeting has begun "; and, finding that such is the case, and insensibly grouping Quaker habits with parliamentary ones, you are obliged to rectify your standard of indoor courtesy, and to accept a new plank in your platform of gentlemanlike behavior.

But presently another observation steals over your senses and fills you with surprise. You had often been assailed with the taunt that your own countrymen monopolized the boorishness of sitting with their feet in such a position as to allow their brains the benefit of gravitation in seeking the head; and you certainly expected that in this assemblage of superlative English gentlemen you would see only dignity and grace of posture. But as the debate goes on you find yourself greatly mistaken; and, in addition to all varieties of grotesque and ungainly lolling, you see one honorable member with his feet raised and resting on the back of the front opposition bench, not more than forty inches from Mr. Disraeli's noble oriental nose; and on inquiry you are amazed to learn that the possessor of the said irreverent feet is neither a parvenu nor a radical, but a good old Tory baronet. When, therefore, you see that even Tory baronets of the old school can sit with their feet up, you are less astonished upon glancing to the other side of the room and finding Whig lords doing the same thing; and you are glad to escape into a consoling reflection, by recalling to mind Fenimore Cooper's dictum that " there is a tendency in the Anglo-Saxon race to put the heels higher than the head."

But something to the credit of House-of-Commons manners I wish to emphasize. In this assemblage of English gentlemen there is one article of furniture that you will not find anywhere—and that is a spittoon! And, what is more to the point, you will not observe any need for one. Oh, my brave countrymen, we have no right to claim the title of freemen until we are free from a certain nefarious habit—a habit which is the product of what Emerson has blandly characterized as the "rage of expectoration"; and, while that habit clings to us, or we to it, we are, and we deserve to be, an abomination to angels and to women, and to the majority of decent men in other countries than our own. It is said of Wilberforce, that on the very night on which the abolition of the slave-trade was carried, and in the midst of the tumultuous congratulations of his friends, he cried out in eager tones, "Well, what shall we reform next?" Perhaps that is a question which we Americans shall have to be asking very soon. At any rate, when slavery in America shall be both dead and buried, and never a tooth or a claw of the monster but is fathoms deep in perdition; and when our mothers, our wives, our sisters, shall have received their full rights at the ballot-box and before the law; and when the currency shall be placed on a sound basis, and the national debt shall be paid, and the tariff question shall be no longer with us—ah, when?—then, at least, we American men shall owe it to ourselves and to our hopes of ever becoming a civilized sex, to inaugurate a new reform—a grand national salivary reform. Certainly, sooner or later we must make a determined effort to adjust ourselves to Sydney Smith's stern and irrevocable verdict: "All claims to civilization are suspended till this secretion is otherwise disposed of. No English gentleman has spit upon the floor since the Heptarchy."

But concerning the personal ways of the House of Commons there are yet some strange things to be told; which, however, I must postpone to another paper.

2 August, 1866.

THE HOUSE OF COMMONS

III

ITS MANNERS

IT is not an idle task, this research of ours into the manners of the House of Commons. After all, manners are the true revealers of man. It is well that Augustine, Rousseau, De Quincey, have given us their confessions; but, could we have looked upon the men themselves, they had been spared this trouble. "Nature tells every secret once. Yes; but in man she tells it all the time—by form, by attitude, gesture, mien, face, and parts of the face, and by the whole action of the machine."

Before you look farther into the behavior of the members of the House of Commons, consider what is the real significance of those personages in this planet of ours. The Queen has almost no direct political power in England; she is only one of England's constitutional fictions — very ornamental and very costly.

The House of Lords is rapidly becoming another constitutional fiction; at this moment its legislative power is reduced to that of criticism, consultation, and passive resistance. In reality, the House of Commons is supreme within the British Empire for all purposes whatsoever. It is king, lords, and commons in one. That you may measure the meaning of such supremacy, glance at these figures:

Number of Members 658
Number of Electors....................1,269,173
Population of United Kingdom........29,321,288
Population of British Empire..........200,000,000
Area of British Empire....4,000,967 square miles.

Thus you are about to approach a committee of six hundred and fifty-eight private English gentlemen, who, through a certain bungling and corrupt hocus-pocus called an election, are, for the time being, the supreme rulers of one fifth of the human family, and one twelfth of the habitable globe.

What was it that I told you a few weeks ago about these gentlemen sitting with their hats on, about their sprawling and ungainly postures, about the elevated condition, if not of their views, at least of their boots? I almost tremble now to think of the audacity of my telltale pen; for did not Aspasia say to Pericles that " the movers and masters of our souls have surely a right to throw out their limbs as carelessly as they please, on the world that belongs to them, and before the creatures they have animated " ? In sooth, these little personal liberties which the members indulge in, these corporeal refractions of the lines of beauty and grace, are but a quiet and harmless way they have of letting their consciousness of imperial authority report itself to the universe, and especially to the strangers' gallery. Certainly they who command one fifth of the human family, and one twelfth of the habitable globe, cannot be expected to obey the professor of deportment.

Besides, the House of Commons is not an assemblage for oratory, or for philosophical discussion, or for dress, or for show of any kind: it is simply a big business committee. And there is something truly admirable in the businesslike plainness, in the commercial simplicity and directness of their ways, in what Charles Lamb would call " the quotidian undress and relaxation " of their state-behavior. It signifies work, not palaver and fuss. They keep their hats on, they put their feet up, they loll about and stretch themselves at full length on their benches, in order to keep alive and extant the idea that that place is not an exhibition-room at all; not a theatric French legislative chamber, with its rostrum for preconcerted declamatory explosions; nor an American Congress, with its writing-desks for members to do their correspondence at, instead of attending to business, and with its animated windmills, going by whiskey and water, grinding out reams of eloquence printed beforehand; but a homely workroom, in which the business of the British Empire is to be industriously transacted.

Nothing could be finer than the tone of quiet, assured strength which on ordinary occasions marks their proceedings; nothing more worthy of imitation than the purpose they manifest of doing the greatest amount of work with the least amount of bluster. Hence it is that they are very impatient under the infliction of eloquence that seems to be going off for its own gratification, and with any orator who is so unfortunate as to betray the fact that he is attacking them with malice prepense and verbose. The sort of man most respected in the House of Commons is he who knows at least one thing, even if he cannot tell it; who works much and says but little about it; while the sort of man least respected there is the professional speech-maker, the senatorial elocutionist, the spouting political geyser.

But there still lingers this question: How about the law of mutual treatment in the

House of Commons? How about that department of manners meant by the word "courtesy"? You have told us how each member treats himself: how does he treat others? This leads us to the great puzzling self-contradictory fact about the House of Commons. In one aspect it is the most courteous, in another the most discourteous, assemblage in the civilized world. Strange! In itself it unites the attributes of almost perfect decorum and of almost perfect indecorum.

The practice of individual courtesy is exquisite. The moment a member rises to address the House, and thus stands forth upon his individual character, he seems possessed by the most refined and gentlemanlike consideration for others. In his allusions to antagonists he carefully guards against the slightest imputation of dishonorable motive; or, if a word of oblique significance should slip from his tongue, he hastens to withdraw it and to express his regret; nay, even in his sarcasms, and home-thrusts, and "argumenta ad hominem," he is careful to mention something to the credit of the very foeman he is about to scathe. Such a thing as casting vituperative epithets, as giving the lie, as threatening personal violence, would not be tolerated in the House of Commons for the fraction of a second, except, indeed, under dire compulsion, in the course of an Irish debate. In this respect, it must be pronounced the finest legislative body known to history. It has brought to the highest perfection the fine art of transfusing exciting debate with those graceful amenities which are twice honorable and also twice blessed, and which lift its discussions leagues above the hot and scurrilous word-brawls into which most men fly when they attempt to argue. There was, for example, nothing approaching it among the ancients. Those statuesque orators of Athens and Rome, of whose glories we have all declaimed at the primary school on Wednesday afternoons, did not at all understand what we may now describe as the English parliamentary mode of debate; they seemed never able to discuss a question without getting extremely red in the face, and calling each other such names as, I dare be sworn, those amiable ladies I yesterday saw selling fish at Billingsgate Market would have exulted in adding to their already copious and vigorous vocabularies. The truth is, the classical method of argumentation was in the utmost measure coarse, abusive, scandalous; while the occasional physical encounters of the ancient statesmen may fill up our cup of bitterness as we are forced to moderate the reverence for their antique grandeur with which in our boyhood we were nobly smitten. What can be said, for instance, on behalf of this piece of Roman majesty? Metellus begins to read aloud to the people the law for the recall of Pompey; but Cato snatches the document away from him. Then Metellus proceeds to recite the law from memory; whereupon Minucius stops his mouth with his hand. Of course, it cannot be agreeable for us, in this connection, to refer to the rampant barbarisms which our American Congress has often witnessed heretofore, and may perhaps often witness again; for, I believe, we are, in some respects, more classical than the classics, and neither Plutarch nor Nepos can furnish us with any ancient hero fit to hold the candle to our Bully Brooks and to our Bully Rousseau. Certainly it is devoutly to be wished that we might impart to all our political discussions the spirit of civility which now, at least, characterizes the House of Commons. The mild statement will even yet bear to be made among us, that a senator is not essentially improved as a debater because he happens to be a blackguard. Wholesome vigor in expression is not necessarily enfeebled by total abstinence from polemical mud-throwing. Real intellectual blows, logical hard-hitting, the stern cut-and-thrust of mind with mind—these are beneficial, the more the better; but they are not rendered more beneficial by being expressed with vulgarity and discourtesy. The immense prestige of

Lord Palmerston enabled him to indulge in many personal liberties in debate, but it never enabled him to indulge in the liberty of being uncivil to the most insignificant or the most unpopular member of the House. When, on one occasion, he said impatiently of Joseph Hume, " If the honorable gentleman's understanding is obtuse, it is not my fault," he was instantly brought to his senses by the reproachful murmurs which rose from all sides of the House, and he was reminded that even Lord Palmerston could not be allowed to forget the fine code of legislative chivalry established there.

But the strange thing about House-of-Commons civility is, that when any member ceases to speak, and subsides from his individual responsibility into the general mass, then, instead of being any longer the incarnation of courtesy, he may, without violating any law or habit of the House, become instantly the incarnation of discourtesy. Standing, he must observe the gracious amenities of debate; sitting, he may do what he likes. Standing, he must not breathe the slightest suspicion against his antagonist; sitting, he may bellow at his antagonist, bray at him, bark at him, mew at him, squeal at him, crow at him, whistle at him, laugh aloud at him. Standing, he must illustrate the manners of an English gentleman; sitting, he is at perfect liberty to illustrate the manners of a ruffian, a cow, a cat, a dog, an ass, a South Sea Islander, or a baboon. I am not indulging in hyperbole. I am literally describing what I have seen and heard, over and over again, in the recent reform debates. I am, in plain language, stating the mode in which high-born, high-bred, and high-titled Tory gentlemen lately received, for example, the speeches of Mr. Gladstone, Lord Hartington, Mr. Layard, and John Bright. I mean merely to say that, in this august assemblage of British legislators in Westminster Palace, you can, on the evening of almost any exciting debate involving class prejudices, hear the most effective speakers perpetually interrupted by noises almost as various and quite as brutish as you could hear at feeding-time in another part of London—namely, at the national collection of wild and tame animals in Regent's Park.

Moreover, this is no late-born custom of Parliament. Miss Martineau mentions a speech made by Henry Brougham forty years ago; and she says that the orator was " interrupted by a peculiar cry, heard amid the cheers of the House, but whether a baa, or a bray, or a grunt, Hansard does not inform us." Brougham himself took notice of the interruption. " By a wonderful disposition of nature," said he, "every animal has its peculiar mode of expressing itself, and I am too much of a philosopher to quarrel with any of those modes." On another occasion, as we are told, a Mr. Wood moved a bill for the admission of dissenters to the universities; but "he could not be heard for the jeering, shouting, coughing, and crowing." The oratory of Daniel O'Connell always had a marvellous effect on the ventriloquial talents of his opponents in the House. Once, when stigmatizing a certain bill as a measure for trampling on the liberties of the Irish, he was met by the usual argument— that is, by jeers, yells, crows, cat-calls, and whistlings. Thereupon he repeated the assertion. Instantly they repeated the interruption. He uttered the assertion a third time. They interrupted a third time. Then the fiery Daniel drew back, and, getting together his Celtic thunderbolts, he launched upon his antagonists these words: "If you were ten times as beastly in your uproar and bellowing as you actually are, I should still feel it to be my duty to interpose to prevent this injustice." Thereupon there was silence in the Tory portion of heaven for the space of half an hour—or less.

England is the far-renowned land of anomalies; but where, even in England, can you find an anomaly so grotesque and so crazy as this, that her legislature should exhibit at once the most opposite qualities—that it should be the most polite and at the same time the most impolite congregation of law-makers ever brought together? It is a sort of millennium of incongruities: here the lamb and the hyena, civility and savagery, lie down together.

14 September, 1866.

MR. DISRAELI

WHEN Dr. Johnson lay dying in Bolt Court, a young Jew named Isaac Disraeli left at his door a manuscript poem, with the somewhat inopportune request that the venerable critic would deign to glance his eye upon it and give judgment concerning its merits. The father of this young Jew was a rich merchant, who had come from Venice to London in 1745; and, as we are informed by his illustrious biographer, he had derived his idea of poets from a print of Hogarth's which represents one of that thriftless tribe as sitting in a garret, inditing an Ode to Riches, while he is being dunned for his milk-score. It was, therefore, with a mixture of shame and of rage that the merchant heard that his own son Isaac had taken the preliminary step to join the impecunious brotherhood. "The loss of one of his argosies uninsured could not have filled him with a more blank dismay." Without a moment's hesitation, and in the hope of curing him of his poetical malady, the merchant hurried the stripling away to a school at Amsterdam; from which, however, the lad in a year or two returned so slightly improved, that, on being informed that a stool was waiting for him in a counting-room at Bordeaux, he replied that on no account could he think of accepting the said stool at Bordeaux, and for this precious reason—that he had already written and was about to print a long poem against Commerce, wherein he had rhythmically imprecated that branch of human enterprise as the great corruptor of mankind. The cup of paternal anguish was now filled to the brim; but with characteristic persistency the old man resolved to try the effects of a journey on his deluded offspring—probably supposing that poetry was a disease somewhat like dyspepsia, to be shaken out of its victim by continuous jolting in a stage-coach. Alas, this remedy proved no more efficient than the other! For, in 1788, Isaac came back to London and gave to the world his poem on "The Abuse of Satire." This production did not succeed in reforming the abuse of satire; but it procured for its author the friendship of Pye, the poet, afterward the poet-laureate, who succeeded in persuading the old merchant to let Isaac stay among his books. And thus it was that for the next half-century the world saw the growth of perhaps the most ardent and the most methodical bibliomaniac that ever lived; and thus it was that we all got the inheritance of those most delightful of gossiping tomes, the "Curiosities of Literature," the "Calamities of Authors," the "Quarrels of Authors," and the "Amenities of Literature." And here in Bloomsbury Square—but a little way from the British Museum, that magnificent and hospitable home of the world's books and the lovers of them—was born unto this glorious book-lover an only son, who, against almost every conceivable disadvantage of position, against the deep, immitigable antagonism of gentile prejudice, has pushed his way by sheer force of brain and of will to be the leader of the aristocratic party in the British House of Commons, the Right Hon. Benjamin Disraeli, now for the third time Chancellor of the Exchequer.

The career of Disraeli the Younger, as he used to be proud of styling himself, will stand as one of the romances of the nineteenth century. He is himself his own greatest novel. His present political and personal attitude in England is something quite unique; and to depict it graphically, and yet with the just gradations of shade and color, is a task for a firmer hand and a more delicate touch than I can pretend to be the possessor of.

In the Chamber of the House, in the committee rooms, in the lobbies, Mr. Disraeli appears often, but he appears like no other member. Above the average height; finely proportioned; invariably dressed with an ostentatious care and with a richness of fabric unusual among Anglo-Saxon statesmen; his hair hanging in long locks of glistening jet upon his brow and neck; with a face of marble—cold, intellectual, haughty, imperious, persistent, stamped with the ineffaceable stamp of the Jew, and trained by years of grim discipline to remain impassive and impenetrable before the keenest stare; Mr. Disraeli bears himself as if companionless in a Parliament where he has sat for twenty-nine years; and as if without a friend in the party which for nearly twenty years he has led with an unquestioned sway. Among the members of the House, even of opposite politics, there is an evident interchange of good fellowship; and to other great party chieftains their squires and henchmen seem bound by personal sympathy and devotion. Last session it was observed, with much amusement, that on one occasion Sir John Pakington, the great Tory assailant of John Bright, crossed the House and sat down upon the gangway steps, at the very feet of his Radical foe, and carried on with him a long and merry conversation; and if toward the member for Birmingham even his arch-antagonist could show such personal cordiality, it may be imagined what must be the display of it on the part of that member's followers and friends. Mr. Gladstone, too, Mr. Mill, Lord Stanley, Mr. Lowe, seem to stand in an atmosphere of friendly reciprocity with the general mass of the members on both sides of the House. Even Mr. Roebuck, that distempered and splenetic soul, that antic compound of the philosopher and the porcupine, seems to be not wholly without personal connections among his brethren. I have seen him hobble along the front of the Liberal benches, and drop a joke into Mr. Gladstone's ear—an ear into which the very next minute he would have been perfectly ready to drop boiling lead. But Mr. Disraeli is the great political solitary, the hermit at the head of the House of Commons! Making no advances to others, others making no advances to him, his unanswering eyes directed straight onward, seeing nothing and yet seeing everything, he moves through the crowds in the lobby with a strange, stealthy, tiger-like, scornful gait, as if each step were the subject of a measurement made ages ago, and each sinuous vibration of his body the fulfilment of a calculation drawn from the depths of a profound policy. About Mr. Disraeli there is nothing spontaneous, nothing accidental. He never so far forgets himself as to have an impulse. He impresses you with having planned and plotted every minutest thing about him—the position of each particular hair, the direction of the tag of each shoe-string, every pulse-throb, every heaving of his lungs. In looking at him, you cannot dismiss the analogy of the tiger; as he glides along the marble floor, you almost expect him to give a spring and to pounce upon his victim. It is hard to see what chance an assassin would ever have with Mr. Disraeli. You cannot doubt that, from a million invisible watch-towers upon his person, he would be warned of the lurking danger, and that he would see and dodge the bullet when in full career.

In the House, too, while other members chat and laugh and exchange greetings, Mr. Disraeli enters with the same cool, deliberate, insinuating shuffle; takes his seat with solemn pomp; places his hat by his side, folds his arms across his bosom, and there sits with scarcely a movement, it may be for hours together. Other members get tired, and show it; Mr. Disraeli seems not to know the meaning of fatigue. Other members yawn, and gape, and stretch their arms, and relieve the tedium of a long sitting by an endless variety of postures; Mr. Disraeli never yawns and gapes, never stretches his arms, has but one posture. Like the race from which he springs, he moves among men without being of them; he deals with their affairs without dealing with them; and when he seems most wrapped in thought, and to have utterly closed the gateways of observation, you cannot doubt that not a sound escapes him, that not a movement of the humblest member but reports itself to the unseeing sentinels in ambush beneath his eyelids. All this isolation is evidently the result of a cherished purpose; the artifice of the most artificial of men. His abstracted air is only an air; he is merely abstracted upon practising the art of seeming abstracted. If Mr. Disraeli were asked why he thus dwells apart, even when most in company, freezing and slaying the first approaches of a warmer personal intercourse, I can fancy him replying in the very words of an old Venetian merchant, who may have been personally known to Mr. Disraeli's ancestors, even if not himself one of them:

> "I'll not answer that;
> But say it is my humor."

It seems to fit his sullen, proud, subtle, Mephistophelian temper to be wrapped in this affectation of mystery, to create this isolation in the House of Commons, to be self-banished to this Sahara of his own ambition.

No one in England now denies that Mr. Disraeli is a man of prodigious talent. With only the education which could be acquired at a private academy in the suburbs of London, at sixteen articled as a clerk to a solicitor, by the time he was of age he had produced the romance of " Vivian Grey," which, by its wit, its polished and brilliant satire, its acute delineations of character, and its poetical imagery, took by storm not only the English public but continental nations also, into whose languages it was at once translated. From that moment a celebrated man, he spent the succeeding ten years of his life in travel, in study, in writing novels, poems, and political tracts, and in frantically trying to get into the House of Commons.

Just how he looked in those early days, just what was then the public estimate of him, may partly be guessed from an etched portrait done by Alfred Croquill for " Fraser's Magazine " some forty years ago. It cleverly intimates the affectations of an oriental coxcomb, then scarcely out of his teens, but already famous for his genius, his impudence, and his foppery. What a picture this is! What marvels of effect are here wrought by a few simple lines! There stands before us, in the immortality of these slender strokes upon the paper, an all-accomplished dandy, with ambrosial curls, with big, poetic eyes, and adorned with ruffles, rosettes, and rings. The life of that graceful voluptuary, for some forty years since then, lends a dangerous plausibility to the belief that it takes a good deal of a man to make a good deal of a fop. Great heroes, statesmen, thinkers, orators, poets, seem now and then to leap out of bandboxes. They are clubs of Hercules, done up in velvet, and dangling with nosegays.

It was in the course of his early and futile attempts to become a member of Parliament that he coquetted with the Radical party, even announcing himself as a Tory-Radical—a title not to be understood without much elucidation. Mr. Disraeli actually made his first appearance as a candidate with credentials from Joseph Hume, W. J. Fox, and Daniel O'Connell; and it was in consequence of his speedy rupture with O'Connell that he stigmatized the agitator as "an incendiary," "a bloody traitor," and "a liar in action and in word," which gave occasion to O'Connell's celebrated taunt that "for aught he knew Mr. Disraeli was a lineal descendant from the impenitent thief on the cross."

In 1837 Mr. Disraeli reached the long-sought goal—a seat in Parliament. I have just been turning over the pages of "Hansard" for that year, and have been reading Disraeli's first speech, which, on the whole, seems to have been the most portentous collapse in oratory that man ever survived. The speech, at least in intention, was a fierce onslaught upon O'Connell. The failure came from no lack of words, but from excess of them. It was a wild, chaotic, fantastic howl—an insane explosion of bombast, literature, nonsense, philosophy, fun, and fury, and was presently stifled in the derisive laughter of the House. Never, perhaps, since the world began had a man made such a fool of himself; and never after, perhaps, till the end of the world, was Mr. Disraeli to have a rival in that kind. As he took his seat, however, he fiercely ejaculated, " I shall sit down now, but the time will come when you will hear me "; a threat fulfilled with even poetic vengeance, when, in 1852, he first became Chancellor of the Exchequer, and, clad in the same garments he had worn at the time of his renowned failure, delivered to a densely crowded assemblage the most brilliant and the ablest budget speech that had been heard there since the days of William Pitt.

It took Mr. Disraeli seven years to atone for his first speech. At last, in 1844, he decidedly gained the ear of the House; and within the next three years, by his incomparably brilliant invectives against Sir Robert Peel, he won his great reputation for elegant, torturing, terrific, parliamentary sarcasm. Those speeches against Peel he has never since equalled; not from loss of faculty, but from loss of victim. They are masterpieces of brilliant, artistic, intellectual, and political vivisection. They are in oratory what the "Letters of Junius" are in journalism. Since that date a great recognized power in the House of Commons, Disraeli is always heard with close attention, often with delight and wonder, never with enthusiasm. Passionless, self-poised, analytic, acute, cunning, critical, he is a perfect master of argumentative fence, and, as John Bright once pronounced him, the ablest Opposition chieftain in the world. One often hears the prediction that, on his next retirement from office, he will accept the honor which has long awaited him —a seat in the Upper House, and the title of the Earl of Hughenden.

There fell from my pen a moment since, with respect to Disraeli, the word "genius." But has Disraeli genius? Well, if he have not genius, he has the art of exhibiting something so nearly like it that millions are of opinion that he has it. If the metal of which he is made be not genuine gold, then it is this new imitation, which they call Milton gold, and which can only be distinguished from the real article by the weight. Nevertheless, as I think, for his purely literary merits, Disraeli does not just now get his full deserts. He has three or four different reputations for as many different kinds of greatness; and these naturally outshine one another; at least, each creates a brightness in which the others are somewhat dimmed.

It is quite the fashion here at present to say, that no man can really understand English politics, or Mr. Disraeli as an English politician, without reading his political novels, more especially " Coningsby." For one, I do not doubt the truth of this statement, but I would add to it that, for the same and for several other good reasons, one should read all of the literary works of this dazzling Jew, in the order in which he wrote them. In this way, at least, we may trace the growth of his mind and style, and perhaps ascertain the weight of his power. Disraeli is full of intellectual tricks, and surprises, and feats of literary legerdemain; yet there is a mine of infinite amusement and suggestiveness in what he has written. I should like to know where you can find anything richer in wit of a very brilliant kind than in his two little dramas,—" Ixion in Heaven," and " The Infernal Marriage." But they are both as audacious and as wicked as they are witty. One of the characters in " The Infernal Marriage " has a striking resemblance to the author, both in sentiment and in the gift of epigram: " For my success in life." says Tiresias, " it may be principally ascribed to a very simple rule— I never trust any one, either God or man."

Of course you should begin as a reader, just where Disraeli began as a writer—with "Vivian Grey." Remember that he sent it flashing into the world when he was but twenty. You will see juvenility in it, to be sure,—but juvenility of the smartest sort. As the evolution of a story, I think it is only a partial success. It has one fatal fault,—it breaks square off in the middle, and then tries to go on again. You get intensely interested in the fortunes of Vivian until, about half-way through the book, he magnificently gets into a duel. At that point the story comes to a head and bursts; and all the rest of it is but a laborious and futile effort at picking up the pieces. But that the stripling who wrote this book had, like its hero, "a devil of a tongue," is shown by such sentences as these, which are only a few of those which one could cite in proof of this statement: "To be a great lawyer, I must give up my chance of being a great man." "Vivian," said his father, "beware of endeavoring to become a great man in a hurry,"—advice which neither Vivian nor Benjamin thought it best to take. "Power is that for which real men should alone exist." "If you wish to win a man's heart, allow him to confute you." "Enemies, in my opinion, are the vulgarest of all possessions."

Of all the novels of Disraeli, none has given

me quite so much delight as have " The Young
Duke," " Contarini Fleming," and " Henrietta
Temple." They all have wondrous vivacity,
rapid dramatic movement, wit, wisdom, tenderness, and a subtile, diffused moral instructiveness. In " Alroy " we have an historical
novel,—a type of novel at which Disraeli himself used to sneer until he tried it. He sneered
with good reason, if there were no historical
novel better than his own. His success in this
department is such as to make other people
sneer at it too! In " Sybil " there is much to
captivate and interest one; and yet as a work
of art the story has many defects. The delineations of character are fainter than is usual
with him; the personages merely touch and go;
the reader is kept on the edge of excitement,
but is not excited; the action is so managed as
to shut off the attention just as it approaches
the interesting points. When you have raced
through a few of these novels, you will conclude that Disraeli, like his early model, Lord
Byron, wrote books in which to paint portraits
of himself. There is an essential identity in
the heroes of his novels. The Young Duke is
only Vivian Grey raised to the peerage; Contarini Fleming is the union of them both in the
poetic temperament; and all are the author
himself.

The great perplexity which you have in trying to make up your mind about Disraeli's greatness, comes from the fact that he himself forbids you to do so. On one page you find something so clever that you are sure he is a genius; but turn over, and you begin to doubt whether he be not a fool. Not seldom do you come upon a passage where it is hard to say whether he is making an ass of himself, or merely assuming that his reader is one.

Ingenious, witty, brilliant, of perfect culture, enriched with ample stores both of solid and of shining learning, an astute politician, a consummate debater, a novelist, a poet, an historian, Benjamin Disraeli would have deserved to be called a great man, if Nature, in giving him that superb intellect, had not at the same time forgotten to give him a conscience and a heart. Or, is this judgment too severe? Perhaps, after all, Mr. Disraeli may have both a conscience and a heart, accompanied, of course, by an astonishing skill in concealing the fact—except from his most intimate friends. Very likely, after he is gone, some of these intimate friends will come forth and tell us all about it; when, possibly, we shall have much occasion to abjure our rash and inadequate conceptions of him.

24 September, 1866.

LORD BROUGHAM

LORD BROUGHAM'S career seems like one long appeal to the sense of astonishment. Not that the things he has done in life have been in themselves of such astonishing merit; but it has been his fortune, or his knack, that, while his exploits in literature, in oratory, and in conduct should be intrinsically noteworthy, they should also, from some extrinsic circumstances, be positively wonderful. Whether intentionally or not, his success has illustrated, in its application to human beings, the principle of wonder-working which Dr. Johnson expounded in the case of dogs: "The wonderful thing about seeing a dog walking on two legs is not that he walks on two legs so well, but that he can walk on two legs at all."

In early life Lord Brougham did what was marvellous because it was done by one so young; in middle age he did things which were marvellous because they were known to have been done amid the appalling multitude of the occupations which his middle age delighted to absorb; in later life he has done things which were marvellous because they were done in later life. In youth he had the maturity of advanced years; in advanced years he has the activity of youth. A venerable boy, a juvenile old man, at each extreme of life he has amazed the world by doing what would not have been amazing at the other extreme; while his stormy middle age was one tremendous Olympian struggle for prizes of all sorts—a multifarious agon for both soul and body, amazing the world because its work was achieved as the facile task of a man who was believed to have but one head and but one pair of hands.

Thus, astonishing one generation by his precocity, another by his versatility, and a third by his antiquity in so wonderful a state of preservation, he seems bent on going down to posterity in person, contending with each successive generation for the fame of having known somewhat of everything, of having done somewhat of everything, of having said a good deal of everything, of having never rested and never got tired, of having been old when he was young and young when he was old!

Nearly thirty years ago, when the splendor of his political and personal renown was under an eclipse—an eclipse, by the way, from which it has not yet emerged—the announcement fell like a crash of thunder out of a clear sky that

Lord Brougham was dead. Personal dislike paused; partisan hostility arrested its own dagger; and the journals of England, with but two notable exceptions, poured forth columns of generous eulogy. When they had given sufficient vent to their lamentations and their praises, his lordship, to their infinite disgust, as suddenly reappeared upon the scene, and in anything but the plight and bearing of a dead man. I think those laudatory journalists never forgave him for coming to life again; and that, if after that event he had had the weakness to die in reality, they would have seasoned their second obituaries with such stuff as would have made him quite contented to stay dead. In fact, it may be imagined that it is from some apprehensions of editorial vengeance of this very kind, that his lordship still persists in refusing them the opportunity of bringing out what they have written about him since his previous death! But it is a curious proof of the sort of reputation Lord Brougham has made for himself in the world that he—the great statesman, judge, orator, philanthropist, philosopher—should have been thought capable of the vanity and the artifice of himself starting the ruse, in order to taste beforehand the verdict of posterity. It has been the fortune of other eminent men to have been proclaimed dead while still in a state of prosperous health;

as, for example, of Gibbon, who, on hearing the report of his own death, instantly wrote off to his friend, Lord Sheffield, an argument to prove that the report was true; but no one that I remember, except Lord Brougham, has ever been suspected of actually starting such a report concerning himself. In the admiration which intelligent Englishmen feel for his great gifts, his great attainments, his great services, for his intellectual vigor, his endurance, his industry, his versatility, his once magnificent eloquence, his philanthropy so fruitful in grand results, there is ever perceptible the impression that he is after all only a splendid showman— that he is nothing unless ostentatious; that his oratory, his mathematics, his chemistry, his natural theology, his legal lore, are for exhibition; that even his joy in the amelioration of society is palpably excelled by his joy in the glorification of Lord Brougham; and that, in addition to being a man of inordinate vanity, he is, partly for this very reason, a man of an unsound judgment and of an untrustworthy moral character. In what is called society in London, the personal veracity of Lord Brougham is not only below par, but below zero—it is never mentioned but to be laughed at, and the one word most derogatory to a gentleman is freely and openly applied to him. In endeavoring to portray the sort of mixed fame which he possesses among discriminating Englishmen, I should perhaps state the case not unjustly by saying that he has their admiration, without their confidence or their love. Lothrop Motley, with very droll effect, mentions that William of Orange regarded Casimir with "respectful contempt." It is very much that kind of regard which Englishmen cherish for Lord Brougham.

I gladly turn to another part of my subject. Whatever may be Lord Brougham's faults, whatever may have been his motives, his career has been one not only of extraordinary brilliance but of extraordinary usefulness. To say nothing of his performances in science and in literature; to say nothing of that powerful forensic eloquence of his, before which even Canning quailed, which nearly shook George IV. from his throne, which made Harry Brougham for twenty-five years the idol of the English people, which rendered him the true successor of Fox, Burke, and Pitt, and which made Lord Palmerston in recent years describe him as the greatest debater heard in Parliament since the first decade of the nineteenth century; he has been connected as leader and advocate with the grandest and most beneficent measures of advancing civilization which have distinguished the past sixty years—with the reform of English law, the repeal of religious disabilities, the abolition of slavery, the establishment of mechanics' institutes, and the extension of political rights to his fellow-countrymen—in short, with all the great measures which have a tendency to make mankind wiser, freer, happier.

It is indeed strange that, even this last week, at Manchester, we should have been hearing long and vigorous speeches from this wonderful old man; that we should have seen on the platform, in the discussion of our very modern themes, and in the company of our very modern men, like Thomas Hughes and Professor Fawcett, a man who was born when the great Napoleon was only ten years old, who was himself two years old when Lord Cornwallis surrendered at Yorktown, who was celebrated in the scientific world three years before the death of George Washington, who, with young Sydney Smith, young Jeffrey, and young Horner, helped to establish the "Edinburgh Review," who wrote in it the contemptuous criticism upon the juvenile poetry of Lord Byron which called forth "English Bards and Scotch Reviewers," who was in full career and widely known in the world before Louis Napoleon, Bismarck, Chief-Justice Chase, General Grant, and Abraham Lincoln had arrived in it.

Of some men it has been sadly said, They lived too soon. Of Lord Brougham, it must be said, with equal sadness, He lived too long. "Better would it have been for him," said Washington Wilks, at the farewell breakfast in London to Henry Ward Beecher, "if Lord Brougham years ago had known how to gather the mantle of his greatness about him and sink down into dignified repose. Since 1848 he has been but the echo of his old renown." For Lord Brougham's fame, perhaps the worst thing that ever happened was that the announcement of his death in 1839 was a ruse.

12 October, 1866.

EARL RUSSELL

THE fame of this venerable statesman—a fame that can now count the ring-marks of more than fifty years—has illustrated the usual course of all earthly reputations: it has had its fluxes and refluxes, its epochs of splendor and of eclipse. It seems to loom up in the history of this half-century, and among the great and the little men who have made that history, like a cold, noble, solitary mountain, on which, however, you may see at one time the sunshine and at another the shadow resting. It is difficult for Englishmen to speak of him by his later and statelier title; their mouths love the old, familiar name of Lord John Russell—a name they heard around their cradles, a name possessing the charm not only of innumerable political associations, but of that happy mixture of the aristocratic and the homely which goes straight to the warmest corner of the British heart.

Providence bestowed upon Lord John at the

outset of life several capital advantages for his
career—not the least, of course, being his birth
into the Bedford family. We have in American
politics nothing at all corresponding in
degree, and almost nothing in kind, to this
tremendous family element in English political
life. Sydney Smith once said that in England
it is regarded as an impertinence for a man
with less than two thousand a year to have any
opinions of his own. In a similar way it is
still an impertinence in the eyes of multitudes
of English people for any man to aspire to
eminent political station who does not belong
to one of the great titled and historic families
of the kingdom; and, if he but have such a
connection, it is amazing with what unquestion-
ing assent these same people behold his official
advancement, quite irrespective of personal
fitness. Lord John entered the world through
the portals of a family from whom Englishmen
accept politicians as naturally as they do bitter
beer from the Bass family, Irish whiskey from
the Kinahan family, horse-flesh from the Tat-
tersalls, and skittle-balls from the ancient firm
of Mr. Madden. Then, too, his early training
at home seems to have been peculiarly fortunate: it was thorough, generous, religious; and
at the University of Edinburgh, under the
teaching of Dr. Thomas Brown, and especially
of Dugald Stewart, those inherited tendencies

toward liberal opinions which he had as a Russell were confirmed on a basis of scholarship and philosophy. It is impossible to interpret the career of Lord Russell without keeping in view the influence upon his nature—upon the acts and the utterances of his whole life—of what we may call his ancestral consciousness. He belongs to a family which is pledged by sacred blood and by seven generations of history to the doctrine of human rights. Since his first access to the public service he has evidently regarded himself as the representative not of this borough or of that county, but of two centuries of tyrant-hating Russells; and there are perceptible also in him a lofty and heroic tenderness toward popular liberty, a pathos, a fidelity, a transparent consecration, as if the mantle of the martyr, William Lord Russell, cherished as a saintly heirloom from generation to generation in his family, had given not merely a dignity, but a holiness, to its living possessor. This is only another way of stating what has been somewhat facetiously said by George Henry Francis, that Earl Russell " always looks at political subjects through the eyes of his ancestors."

Entering the House of Commons in 1813, at the age of twenty-one, he at once identified himself with those men and those measures that seemed to be tending in the direction of progress; but after three years of parliamentary service, in a mood of deep depression at the apparently unassailable supremacy of Toryism in England, he came to the resolution of withdrawing from political life. From this course, however, he was dissuaded by the strenuous appeals of his friends, particularly of Thomas Moore. Taking a fresh start, with courage reinvigorated, he set steadily at work to fight out Toryism on that line. Against the cruel repressive measures of the government, against Catholic disabilities, against religious disabilities of all sorts, against the slave trade, against the monstrous anomalies of the English electoral system, he strove year after year, with persevering work, by speeches, by books, by votes. In 1819 he first introduced his celebrated resolution for representative reform; and that resolution, sneered at, ridiculed, voted down, he brought to the House every year thereafter until 1831, when the movement, which he had so long promoted and of which he seemed the impersonation in the Lower House, culminated in the great reform bill.

The attempt has been made, partly by ignorant persons and partly by jealous ones, to rob Earl Russell of the honor of his peculiar association with that great act of political redemption—that act which, as has been remarked by an admirable English writer, " will be to thoughtful students a thousand years hence what Magna Charta is to us." For example, Mr. Roebuck, who has written a history of the reform bill, and who hates Lord Russell, said a few weeks ago, in a speech at Sheffield, that it was preposterous for Earl Russell to claim conspicuous credit in connection with that celebrated measure, and applied to him the fable of the fly on the wheel. To satisfy one's self, however, as to the relation of Earl Russell to the first reform bill, it is only necessary to turn to the parliamentary debates and to the newspapers of the period, and to observe how conspicuous Lord John Russell was as an object both of attack and of eulogy; how, for instance, the bill was assailed by Sir Charles Wetherell as "Russell's Purge," in ludicrous allusion to Colonel Pride's famous purgatorial treatment of the same House in Cromwell's time; and how, likewise, the bill was extolled in one of the glittering speeches of the young Macaulay as a measure which would give "additional lustre to a noble name inseparably connected during two centuries with the dearest liberties of the English people."

With the triumph of the reform bill Lord John undoubtedly reached the summit of his renown; and it cannot be denied that within a very few years from that event he succeeded in greatly disappointing the expectations that had been formed concerning him. The decay of his popularity was due to several causes. Lord Palmerston, then undervalued, steadily gained upon him in the public estimation, overtook him, passed him, and during the past twenty years not only threw Lord Russell into the shade, but induced the world to overrate himself as decidedly as it had previously underrated him. The death of Lord Palmerston was the signal for the retributive process to begin of restoring these two men to their rightful positions; henceforward every year that passes will reveal more and more clearly that Lord Palmerston was an utterly commonplace character—merely a clever public functionary, jovial, audacious, and time-serving—while the same lapse of years will probably more and more fix the fame of Earl Russell as one of the high, pure, and abiding lights in the firmament of English statesmanship. That Earl Russell lost favor during the Palmerstonian epoch was a reproach not to Earl Russell, but to the epoch. It was but one indication of the decline of earnestness during that time.

I do not mean to convey the impression that Earl Russell is a statesman without imperfections. It is generally asserted here that he has lamentably failed in two very important departments of modern statesmanship—in diplomacy and in finance; and that he lacks the physical and emotional qualities needful to a great leader of men. He is himself a little man, thin, gasping, and cold. Without the personal majesty of Sir Robert Peel; without the heart-power, the merry, blunt, and even affectionate good-fellowship of Palmerston, he inherits the Russell attribute of iciness. If he tries to thank you, he gives you a chill; his attempts at being gracious set your teeth a-chattering. He is the sort of person whom the literary critic of " The Times " lately described as a " peripatetic refrigerator." Besides, though his life has been on the whole a grand testimony to lofty and liberal principle; though in the depths of his being he loves right better than applause and the rewards of office; he has shown, at critical junctures, an infirmity of moral courage and a disposition to catch a momentary huzza by trimming to the popular breeze. Thus, while the anti-corn-law movement was struggling with misrepresentation and contempt, Lord John saluted it as " mischievous, absurd, impracticable, and unnecessary "; but so soon as the movement gave signs of an early triumph, his lordship, with unseemly haste, rushed into its advocacy. Thus, again, during our late struggle, he yielded to this weakness by flattering a superficial English opinion in that famous and damnatory epigram: "The North is fighting for empire; the South for independence." Yet all well-informed persons here knew at the time and throughout the war that the sympathies of Earl Russell were with the national cause, and that he would exult with unfeigned joy in its success.

As an orator, he belongs to that class of men whose orations read better than they sound. Indeed, his speeches can scarcely be said to sound at all. As an orator, he is pre-eminently the great inaudible. I remember that in one account of his first speech on the reform bill, it is mentioned that he was heard with difficulty; and since his attainment of old age and the peerage his vocal energies have fallen to as aristocratic a state of non-existence as if he had sat in the House of Lords all his life. He makes incessant use of the rhetoric of coughing and stammering; he has a marked provincial accent; he crowds his sentences with colloquial and commonplace phrases; yet among this mass of verbal rubbish he deposits gems of fine thought set in language of magical felicity. Many times, too, during his parliamentary career, he has shown skill in repartee of a very high order. For example, on one occasion during the debates on the first reform bill, Sir Francis Burdett, who had been for many years a roaring Radical and in his old age had joined the Conservatives, accused Lord John of indulging in " the cant of patriotism "; when, instantly, his lordship, fixing his eye on the blatant renegade, remarked that " there was also such a thing as the recant of patriotism." Another fine instance of his readiness in reply is given by Molesworth in his " History of the Reform Bill." That bill had been rejected by the House of Commons. The House of Commons was then dissolved and a general election ordered; the result of which was that a new House was returned with an enormous majority in favor of reform. When Lord John stood up to address the new House he said: " It has been charged that the late elections were governed not by reason but by passion." At this remark the Tories set up a great cheer, with the purpose of endorsing the assertion with the emphasis of their most reproachful approval. " That the electors have been moved by passion," continued the speaker, " I will not deny." Then broke from all the Tory benches another and a more tremendous cheer. " Yes," added his lordship triumphantly, " love to one's country is a passion, and by that love the electors have indisputably been moved!" At this happy turn the cheering was of course on the other side of the House.

The eminence of Earl Russell's renown in politics has overshadowed his own fame in literature; yet his labors in the latter sphere have been neither few nor undistinguished. Besides innumerable pamphlets, letters, and speeches, he has published many books: " Life and Correspondence of C. J. Fox," " Memoirs of Thomas Moore," a rhymed tragedy called " Don Carlos; or, Persecution," " Essay on the History of the English Government and Constitution," " Life and Times of Fox," " Life of William Lord Russell," and " Memoirs of the Affairs of Europe from the Peace of Utrecht." The titles of the various publications to which his name is attached cover twenty-eight pages of the catalogue of the British Museum.

Of all the great statesmen of English history who have held high office, he is among the purest; and with all the still greater statesmen of English history who have not held high office he will bear comparison for real nobility of purpose. He is a politician of absolute truth of speech. His long life has been animated and exalted by a grand inspiration. His name will be forever linked with the most important event which has happened in England since 1688. But all his titles to our gratitude and our homage were summed up by John Bright a few weeks ago, and concentrated into a single sentence: " Lord Russell has no fear of freedom." In these ancient lands, where the very air is poisoned by the suspicion of the few with respect to the many, where aristocrats and kings build dykes against the ferocity of mankind as the Dutch do against the ferocity of the ocean, this is indeed the utmost praise that could be bestowed.

6 November, 1866.

JOHN BRIGHT

I

PERSONAL AND POLITICAL TRAITS

IF, at high noon to-morrow, vote were to be taken throughout England, by a show of hands, upon the question of being for or against John Bright, nearly all the hands that would go up against him would be encased in kid gloves, and nearly all the hands that would go up for him would be without gloves of kid or other material. Still John Bright would win the day!

It is decidedly not the fashionable thing here to be a follower of the great Radical statesman. Indeed, is there a country yet discovered on this planet where the people of fashion are on the side of radicalism? In England the dandies are, of course, against John Bright; and so also are the trimmers; and so are the people who put out their thinking to be done for them, as they put out their washing; and, finally, they too are against John Bright who, while doing their own thinking, yet do it from the inspiration of fear rather than from the inspiration of faith. All other classes, so far as I can ascertain, are John Bright people.

We have no statesman in America whose position is exactly like John Bright's in England; for his talents admired by all, for his principles passionately hated by many, passionately loved by more. Charles Sumner's moral pedestal is somewhat like Mr. Bright's. But Mr. Sumner is a great and a severe scholar, while Mr. Bright is not a scholar at all. To paraphrase an English saying, Mr. Sumner is John Bright plus the ability to read Homer. On the other hand, Mr. Bright has all the qualities of a great popular leader; while Mr. Sumner, though a popular teacher, is scarcely a popular leader at all. John Bright's heart beats in his brain, on the tip of his tongue, in the palm of his hand. His presence is witchery; his sway is the delicious despotism of a tremendous charmer; his followers are not only disciples — they are devotees. Still, between the position of Sumner and the position of Bright there is this resemblance: they both, as politicians, appeal especially to the moral sense of their countrymen, and as champions of the depressed classes they both array against themselves the same inevitable antagonism of selfishness, prejudice, timidity, distrust, thoughtlessness, and fashion. Had Wendell Phillips been in the United States Senate for twenty years, and still been Wendell Phillips, he would have been, by his personal geniality, far more exactly than is Charles Sumner, the American John Bright.

By one infallible test we are forced to decide that Mr. Bright is the foremost man now extant in England—he is the most abused man in England. When Dr. Johnson was congratulated on the success of one of his terrific pamphlets against the American colonists, he replied, with a growl, that the pamphlet had not succeeded, that it had not been sufficiently abused, and that for his own part he always estimated the force of a blow by the rebound. The intellectual, the emotional rebound against Mr. Bright in this country is something superb; it constitutes his crown of glory; it leaves him, beyond all rivalry, the supreme Englishman alive. Throughout these islands, every number of every Tory paper, and of every demi-Tory paper, as surely, as systematically flings its little stone, or its little dust, or its little mud at John Bright, as it prints its heading in big letters and its leaders in small ones. It was said of a certain Frenchman that he held his place in Paris society on the tacit understanding that he should be always witty. Fortunately for the Tory papers, no such necessity is laid upon them; but they do hold their places in the Conservative party on the tacit understanding that they shall be always abusive of John Bright. In the House of Commons, too, the case is the same. You would be amazed, on looking over " Hansard," to find what an enormous majority of the parliamentary speeches there embalmed during the last fifteen years contain thrusts at this one man; and you could not sit through an evening's debate on any conceivable subject without being startled by the incessant and spiteful allusions to " the honorable member for Birmingham." Indeed, those five words constitute the one expression most thoroughly stereotyped just now in the vernacular of that assemblage. Its use in a tone of dislike is more than a party shibboleth; it has bloomed into political cant. Meanwhile, John Bright sits there, at the head of the second bench below the gangway, the most undisturbed and the most impregnable-looking man that can be imagined. Of a stout, square, and solid frame, with a broad, open English face, his massive brow shadowed by the wide brim of his hat, with lips firmly compressed by thoughtfulness and determination and carved of that peculiar shape that denotes them the fiery steeds of eloquence, he seems no more concerned in the nightly patter about "the honorable member for Birmingham" than if that celebrated member were a person with whom he was not even acquainted. Indeed, I imagine that these references to himself are positively no longer heard by him, on the principle that sounds oft-recurring and despised come to have no more effect upon the sensorium than sounds not made at all — as the sleepy college-boy at last snores majestically through the diabolical clatter of his alarm-clock and the sacred twang of the prayer-bell.

The spectacle of John Bright in the House of Commons is one of the best things to be seen in this part of the world. For myself, I should not have regretted the voyage across the Atlantic, had it conferred no other happiness than that of a good long look at John Bright sitting in the Parliament of Great Britain: the peerless champion of popular rights — honored though feared among the elegant, scornful, and flippant contemners of popular rights — the kingliness of his towering intellect, the splendor of his Thor-like eloquence, the earnestness of his big, warm, indomitable heart, all impersonated in that noble presence, and all contrasted by the unreality, the chatter, the schoolboy singsong, the petty, nibbling arguments, the vapid, frivolous, unmeaning, unending flow of foppish politics and of aristocratic impertinence, which make up the most of an evening's discussion in that celebrated legislature which Bishop Coxe has rather severely described as "the Senate of Lilliput."

Let no lover of John Bright feel pained to hear that the great Radical is constantly assailed here. These assaults are as harmless upon him as the splash of the dolphin's fins against the ribs of the "Great Eastern." Among all mortal men John Bright is pre-eminently able to take care of himself.

But, while he is thus politically hated—while he is the mark for every verbal brickbat that any Tory arm can fling across the broad aisle— he is said to be personally a great favorite. I am told that in the coffee-room no other member is so soon surrounded by a group of friendly talkers. Indeed, it seems that the conversational fascinations of John Bright are even greater than the fascinations of his public oratory; and that the notablest speeches that ever come out of his lips come out as he sits in the coffee-room, with a cigar in one hand, a glass of sherry in the other, and a crowd of delighted and enthralled political enemies swarming about him.

When, a few years ago, his health gave way and the gravest fears were excited, grief and alarm pervaded all England—not alone the Liberal party. Every post came to him laden with letters of sympathy and regret, from the chiefs of that old nobility against whose political pretensions his whole life has been a battle. Every palace, and castle, and baronial hall in England would have opened its portals to receive and give repose to the man whom all Englishmen know to be one of the greatest masters of the English language, one of the noblest apostles of Christian statesmanship, a fearless, rough, hard-hitting antagonist — an honest man!

19 October, 1866.

JOHN BRIGHT

II

PHASES OF HIS CAREER

JOHN BRIGHT was born at Greenbank, near Rochdale, in 1811. He is thus of the same age as Charles Sumner; two years older than Bismarck and Henry Ward Beecher; twelve years older than General Grant; two years younger than Gladstone; three years younger than Louis Napoleon, Andrew Johnson, General Lee, and Chief-Justice Chase; four years younger than Mill; six years younger than Disraeli; twelve years younger than Lord Derby; nineteen years younger than Earl Russell; and thirty-two years younger than Lord Brougham.

His father was a large manufacturer and cotton-spinner of Rochdale, and the illustrious statesman himself inherits the business and is still principal of the firm of "John Bright & Brothers." Though only just of age during the great reform agitations of 1832, he first breathed his eloquence in that cause. But it was not until 1839 that he rose to distinction, and then as a political orator in the tremendous enterprise of breaking up "the stupid and ignorant monopoly of the landowners" in food. The story of his first connection with that movement and of the birth of his friendship with Mr. Cobden, who was by seven years his senior, is one of the most touching and dramatic in biography. Mr. Cobden, lecturing at Rochdale against the corn laws, had been entertained over night at the house of John Bright's father; and it was on that occasion that he had some conversation with the son, his future colleague. About the same time, also, he heard the son address a public meeting, and was impressed by the force and electric fervor of his oratory. Some time afterward, in 1838, Mr. Cobden found John Bright at Leamington, bowed down in grief over the loss of his young wife. With true spiritual wisdom the apostle of free trade saw not only that the cause needed John Bright, but that John Bright needed the cause; and believing that only in working for others would the mourner find consolation for himself, he addressed to him those words which in this country are now as memorable as Lloyd Garrison's famous declaration is in America: " Come with us, and we will never rest till we have abolished all monopoly." John Bright arose and went; and in his new task he found joy, usefulness, renown. He found also in Mr. Cobden a brother, from whom during life he was parted by no breath nor shadow of alienation, and of whose memory he can now never speak save with faltering voice.

Having acquired fame as a political orator outside of Parliament, Mr. Bright stood for Durham in 1843, and was defeated; but in the latter part of the same year, a vacancy occurring in the same borough, he stood again, and was successful. He represented Durham from that year until 1847; he represented Manchester from 1847 until 1857; in May of the latter year, in consequence of the unpopularity he had braved by his opposition to the Crimean and the Chinese wars, he was defeated at Manchester, being himself absent from England in ill-health; but in the August following he was returned for Birmingham, and has remained a member for that borough ever since. Thus, with the unimportant exception of a few months' banishment, John Bright has now been a member of Parliament for twenty-three years.

The political careers of Russell, Derby, Brougham, and even Gladstone have been achieved in the grooves of favoring circumstances: the political career of John Bright is a defiance of circumstances. He started with scarcely one of the usual outward conditions of English political success: without family influence, without the alliance of the Established Church, without the endorsement of either university. Canning, and Peel, and Gladstone all rose from the middle classes. The first was the son of an actress, the second of a cotton-spinner, the third of a Liverpool merchant. But they all had the aristocratic prestige of an education at Oxford, and they all belonged to the Established Church. Even Mr. Disraeli's case is not in difficulty a parallel to Mr. Bright's. It is true that Mr. Disraeli is not a university man, and yet has succeeded in a country where for ages the two universities have bestowed the badge of social and even of political consideration. It is true that Mr. Disraeli is a Jew, and yet has succeeded in a land where the detestation of Jews is an ineradicable passion. No doubt the race whose image he wears in his face has been a tremendous obstacle to his success; for, as Mr. Hutton has lately said, " the Semitic principle has been in Mr. Disraeli's way all his life, and it is the only principle which has." But while the Jew has conquered, he has conquered by surrendering: he has conciliated the Church by joining her; he has gained the universities by abetting their claims; he has appeased aristocratic prejudice by becoming its champion. Nor can Mr. Cobden be cited as an example of success as great as Mr. Bright's, achieved against odds as great; for the haughty agricultural party never forgot that Mr. Cobden was the son of a farmer, and churchmen never forgot that he was a devout member of their own august Establishment. John Bright the cotton-spinner and the son of a cotton-spinner, John Bright the Quaker, John Bright who probably never saw the inside of either university, is perhaps the first renowned English statesman who has won a great position without any confederation with the three great forces in English political life—marching straight up the face of the hill to the very summit against the combined batteries of social, literary, and ecclesiastical enmity. Among a people with whom Quakers are next to Jews as objects of dislike, the Quaker statesman is master of the situation; in an island whose agricultural aristocracy cherish the maxim that " the nation that builds on manufactures sleeps on gunpowder," the Rochdale manufacturer has become himself an estate of the realm; and in a kingdom where a few years ago, according to Charles Knight, " the admission of a merchant to the councils of the sovereign would have been deemed pollution," the chief of the firm of " John Bright &

Brothers" will soon be a cabinet minister, and have a seat at the table where Her Majesty presides.

John Bright is not only a great statesman; he is a great political phenomenon. His career indicates the uprising of a new power in England. It means that the English people are at last a noteworthy fact in English politics. It means that there are other persons in this country to be taken into consideration than the one hundred and fifty amiable gentlemen who own half the soil of England, or the ten equally amiable gentlemen who own half the soil of Scotland. John Bright is the announcement of a new era for Britain, for Europe—the era not of great families, but of one family greater than the great families, that of MAN!

Though the career of Mr. Bright is so transcendent in England, it has by no means reached its culmination. You may everywhere in these islands hear Englishmen speculating, some with dread, some with joy, as to what he is likely to become in the land. A few days ago Mr. Du Cane, a junior Lord of the Admiralty, addressed his constituents upon the prospect of John Bright playing the part of Oliver Cromwell. On the other hand, you will meet intelligent men who are looking forward to Mr. Bright's accession to power as to the daybreak of a political millennium. John

Bright is a colossal statue; but he is a colossal statue only partially unveiled. It is amusing to observe how long a time it has taken for the veil to come even partially off. It is not without a smile that we now read in a critical work on British statesmen, published twenty years ago, the allusion to two young members of Parliament as " Mr. Cobden and his Sancho Panza, Mr. Bright," and to the latter alone as " a public man whose position is still undefined." There are some respects in which a statesman's position remains undefined until it is defined by death; but I think that, if the critic of 1846 had lived till 1866, he would have been able to get somewhat nearer to a definition of Mr. Cobden's Sancho Panza.

John Bright is a politician of that new and grander school of politics which is to mould the next epoch here and in America—that school which resolves to terminate the monstrous divorce of politics and morals. Henceforth, in both these empires, he only should be recognized as a statesman who bases the doctrine of Policy upon the doctrine of Right. Garrison, Sumner, Chase, on one side of the Atlantic; Bright, Mill, Gladstone, Hughes, Goldwin Smith, Francis Newman, on the other side— these are the high-priests who are to assist in that sacred remarriage of Politics and Ethics.

In England, as has been lucidly explained by

Miss Martineau, there are two parties—" the adherents of things as they were, the advocates of things as they ought to be." Of this latter party—this dawning and conquering party—this party of Faith, and Hope, and Love—John Bright is the great oratorical leader, even as Mr. Gladstone is its great parliamentary leader, as Mr. Mill is its great philosophical leader.

For his advocacy of Christian principles in application to political practice, John Bright has to meet every day of his life, and from hundreds of presses, and from thousands of throats, the accusation of being revolutionary, disloyal, traitorous. In that wonderful speech on Ireland which he made in the House of Commons last February—that speech which Mr. Grant Duff has declared to be the most impressive one delivered in this generation—Mr. Bright took notice of the censure:

" But I have heard from members in this House, I have seen much writing in newspapers, and I have heard of speeches elsewhere, in which some of us, who advocate what we believe to be a great and high morality in public affairs, are charged with dislike to the institutions, and even disloyalty to the dynasty which rules in England. There can be nothing more offensive, nothing more unjust, nothing more utterly false. We who ask Parliament, in dealing with Ireland, to deal with it upon the unchangeable principles of justice are the friends of the people and the really loyal advisers and supporters of the throne. All history teaches us that it is not in human nature that men should be content under any system of legislation and of institutions such as exists in Ireland. You may pass this bill, you may put the home secretary's five hundred men in gaol—you may do all this, and suppress the conspiracy and put down the insurrection ; but the moment it is suppressed there will still remain the germs of this malady, and from those germs will grow up as heretofore another crop of insurrection and another harvest of misfortune."

Those sentences are more than a vindication —they are a sermon. They preach that the employment of " a great and high morality in public affairs " is the true method of putting down "insurrection," and that those statesmen only who act upon " the unchangeable principles of justice " will ever succeed in exterminating the germs of any political malady.

26 October, 1866.

JOHN BRIGHT

III

AS AN ORATOR

THE talking talent is not one of those personal gifts which Englishmen delight to honor. If in America the tendency is to overrate its merit, and to heap exaggerated rewards upon its distinguished exercise, in England there is a tendency quite as pronounced in the opposite direction. It is true that Britons find enjoyment in eloquence, for, after all that can be said about them, Britons are human. They are, indeed, greatly moved by eloquence, and are remarkably demonstrative under its power. But when the performance is over, when the lights are out, the spell broken, and they themselves safely escaped into the cooling air, a reaction commonly sets in, and they are very much inclined to estimate the talent by which they have been so highly entertained as at best only a species of mountebank cleverness. "A mere talker," "a glib tongue," "the gift of the gab"—these are descriptions which in England, and especially among cultivated people, are meant to be the reverse of complimentary. So much is this the case that parliamentary speakers not seldom either affect a hesitant and bungling utterance or are too conscious of the political value of its natural possession to make any effort to overcome it. There is a feeling in the land that very great sincerity must needs talk slowly, and now and then even stumble; that real thoughtfulness can never mount the swifter steeds of speech; that only shallowness and passion and hypocrisy are particularly fluent. Hence bad speaking is really an element of availability. Hence great men, placing themselves at the service of their country, will hem and haw from patriotic and ambitious motives. They will inspire the reverence of their constituents by a judicious blending of coughing, stammering, and logic. They will carry an election or win the honors of a debate by the persuasive manifestation of an inability to talk. Shakespeare's Antony was a very good Englishman, rather than a Roman, when he tried to fasten upon Brutus the stigma of being eloquent: " I am no orator —as Brutus is!"

"Oh, he can speak!" Such was the damnatory verdict on John Bright which came with sneering accent from the curled lips of an English scholar the other day, with whom I happened to be walking out of the library of the British Museum. Nothing else that Thomas Carlyle said to the boys at the University of Edinburgh a few months ago so delighted the English people as those witty sentences against talk which the greatest of living talkers put into that amusing talk of more than two hours' length, on his inauguration as Lord Rector:

"There is very great necessity, indeed, of getting a little more silent than we are. It seems to me the finest nations of the world—the English and the American—are going all away into wind and tongue. Silence is the eternal duty of a man. I must say that speech does not seem to me to have turned to any good account. If a good speaker—an eloquent speaker—is not speaking the truth, is there a more horrid kind of object in creation?"

And straightway Mr. Punch took this last sentence, and gave it the point which so many of its readers had already applied to it, by printing it under a ludicrous cartoon representing John Bright haranguing a begrimed and gaping crowd of artisans.

Nevertheless, as I have already condescended to allow, Britons after all are human; and the love of eloquence is a universal human instinct. Even Britons cannot in all cases with success contend against it. Natural passions are stronger than conventional ones. Thus it has happened, no doubt, that even in a country where, according to Sydney Smith, "an audience is apt to consider the man who tires them less than usual as a trifler and a charlatan," and where, according to Lord Lytton, "Hesitating, Humming, and Drawling are the Three Graces of Conversation," John Bright, by sheer force of oratory, and against the general contempt for oratory, as well as against every disadvantage of religious, educational, and social prejudice, has risen to be not only an unsurpassed personal force in England, but positively one of the institutions of England.

It must be confessed, however, that if English antipathy to oratory has in this case given way, it has done so under a provocation which all the world and succeeding ages will be likely to consider as sufficient to justify so exceptional a procedure. We believe all students of his speeches now admit that John Bright is one of the greatest exemplars of a pure, manly, and commanding eloquence that any age or any language can produce.

There are some great orators whose speeches, though they may be read with delight when printed, fall heavy and dead in the actual delivery. Such an orator, at certain times, was Edmund Burke. On the contrary, there are orators whose speeches produce an amazing effect in the actual delivery, but furnish, when cold in type, extremely dismal reading-matter to the hapless wight who may encounter them. Such an orator was Whitefield; such an orator was Lord Brougham; such an orator was Henry Clay. Indeed a great master of eloquence has by implication made this latter characteristic almost a proof of the excellence of the speech as delivered. " Does the speech read well?" said Charles James Fox, " then, depend upon it, it was a poor one." But is not the perfect orator he whose speech is so fluent yet so thoughtful, so fine in manner yet so choice in quality, so glowing with passion yet so rational, so weighty, so suggestive, that while it sways the vast throng as it leaps from the lips which first give it utterance, it still has, if fairly reported, a charm even for the student in the closet? Such an orator was Daniel Webster; such an orator is Wendell Phillips; such an orator is that noble English statesman whose eloquence now wields the fierce democracy of England.

John Bright has a merit which is not a very common one among our own popular speakers; he uses pure English, avoiding alike the opposite vulgarisms of bombast and of slang. His style is simply perfect: racy, strong, sharp, terse, and clear, with a basis of glorious Saxon coming straight from the market and the hearth, and just enough impregnated with courtly Norman to give it elevation, nobleness, and an occasional majesty and musical pomp. This, his almost infallible taste in the choice of words, is the key to his victory over the orator-scorning fastidiousness of the educated classes of England. "Whence got this Quaker demagogue that marvellous mastery of style which we university men, toiling for it through all ancient and modern lore, would now gladly give our right hands to possess?" Such is the frequent and amazed inquiry of many an English scholar. "I may be nothing," said the orator modestly last year at Rochdale, "only your fellow-townsman, a man not brought up in universities or in the society of statesmen." "I have not had the same advantages which others have had," said the orator in the House of Commons a few weeks afterward, "but that fact only makes me the more value that which others have obtained." It is still common for public speakers in England, and especially in the House of Commons, to quote from the Greek and Roman classics, and such quotation is still considered to be what Dr. Johnson called it, "the watchword of literary men." John Bright never tries to utter the scholastic shibboleth. I do not remember a Latin sentence, and scarcely a Latin word, in any of his speeches, and I am sure he never spoke a Greek one. But he partly reveals the character of his favorite studies as well as the source of his exquisite English vocabulary, by the snatches of English poetry which he occasionally introduces into his speeches, and always with aptness and impressive effect.

I shall not soon forget with what sweetness, in speaking of the brightening effect of a true Sunday on the toiling classes of Lancashire, he once quoted a couplet of George Herbert's:

> " The week were dark without thy light ;
> Thy torch doth show the way."

I have never listened to anything finer of its kind than a passage in a very grand speech which I had the privilege of hearing him make, a few weeks ago, in the town hall at Birmingham. He was describing the progress of popular liberty in the English colonies and in the United States, and then, returning to Europe, he said:

" You will find in the republic of Switzerland, in the kingdoms of Holland and Belgium, in Norway, in Sweden, in France, and now in Germany also, a wide spread exercise of the franchise hitherto unknown in our time in this country ; and neither emperor nor king nor noble believes that his authority or his interest, his own greatness or the happiness of any of his countrymen will be jeopardized by the free admission of the people to the constitutional privileges. What is it that we are come to in this country, that what is being rapidly conceded in all parts of the world is being persistently and obstinately refused here in England—the home of freedom, the mother of parliaments——"

At this point the orator paused, as if struggling for some loftier and more vivid language with which to portray the peculiar glory and, therefore, the peculiar shame of England, and then in an instant he resumed, as these fine lines from Addison seemed to flash upon his memory—

"of which one of her own poets has said,

'Though o'er our heads the frozen Pleiads shine,
'T is Liberty that crowns Britannia's isle,
And makes her barren rocks and her bleak mountains smile.'"

It was but an audience of workingmen, yet the splendor of the quotation and its application to the argument, all the more powerful because so delicate, were fully appreciated, and the vast assemblage seemed lifted from their seats by their enthusiasm. But when the next morning that speech was laid on every aristocratic breakfast-table in England, and innumerable eyes, that could but sparkle at literary excellence, fell upon this passage, with what a tantalized mixture of fury and delight would many a Tory squire and nobleman exclaim: " The Quaker dog! Where did he get such English? And now, see! he has broken into the very armory of our poets, has stolen their choicest weapons, and is using them to knock our brains out!"

In closing the last speech he ever made, Mr. Cobden said, " I never perorate." It may be said of his illustrious friend, Mr. Bright, that he never closes a speech without perorating. Of course I do not mean that even he perorates in the exact sense which Mr. Cobden meant—that of an elaborated strain of ostentatious rhetoric. But Mr. Bright has what Mr. Cobden had not —an oratorical temperament; and as he draws towards the conclusion of a speech his mind seems to rise to a grander and more kindling view of his theme; he sweeps over the whole a more burning glance; and, as if exulting in the amplitude of his own resources for expression, he gathers them up and pours them forth at last in his richest and most energetic sentences. An admirable instance of this habit, and one which illustrates, also, many of the best qualities of his manner, was the peroration of his magnificent speech for the reform bill in the House of Commons last April:

"I have been misrepresented and condemned and denounced by honorable gentlemen opposite, and by not a few writers in their press. My conscience tells me that I have labored honestly only to destroy that which is evil, and to build up that which is good. The political aims of the last twenty-five years, as they were summed up the other night by the honorable member for Wick, are my political aims, if they can be called the aims in any degree of any living Englishman. And if now, in all the great centres of our population,—in Birmingham with its business districts, in Manchester with its encircling towns, in the population of the West Riding of Yorkshire, in Glasgow and amidst the vast industries of the West of Scotland, in the great Babylon in which we are assembled—if we do not find ourselves surrounded by hungry and exasperated multitudes—if now, more than at any time during the last hundred years, it may be said, quoting the beautiful words of Mr. Sheridan, that

'Content sits basking on the cheek of toil,'—

if this House and if its statesmen glory in the change, have I not as much as any living statesman some claim to partake of that glory? I know, and every thoughtful man among you knows, and those gentlemen who sit on that bench and who are leading you to this enterprise, they know that the policy I have urged upon the House and upon the country, so far as it has hitherto been accepted by Parliament, is a policy conservative of the public welfare, strengthening the just authority of Parliament, and adding from day to day fresh lustre and dignity to the Crown. And now when I speak to you and ask you to pass this bill—when I plead on behalf of those who are not allowed to speak for themselves in this House—if you could raise yourselves for this night, for this hour, above the region of party strife—if you could free yourselves from the pestilent atmosphere of passion and prejudice which so often surrounds us here, I feel confident that at this moment I should not plead in vain before this imperial Parliament on behalf of the English constitution and the English people."

30 October, 1866.

JOHN BRIGHT

IV

AS AN ORATOR

THE only living Englishman who can be spoken of as a rival in eloquence of John Bright is Mr. Gladstone. Upon the question, so often discussed in England, of their comparative merits, Louis Blanc has given an opinion which, very characteristically, is both a verdict and an epigram: "Mr. Gladstone would be the first orator in England were there no Mr. Bright, and although there is a Mr. Bright, Mr. Gladstone is unquestionably the first orator in the House of Commons." In thus awarding the palm to Mr. Gladstone for parliamentary eloquence, and to Mr. Bright for the sort of eloquence which is most effective with a popular assemblage, the brilliant French exile has no doubt expressed the general conclusion of English society, though I am inclined to think that it is a conclusion which will not be entirely confirmed by the next generation.

Aside from any comparison between the two men, if we take a critical inventory of Mr. Bright's stock of faculties as contributing to his success in oratory, we shall not get far on without perceiving that his greatest faculty is the faculty of keeping all his other faculties in poise. He has imagination; he has courage; he has art, humor, sarcasm, the gift of invective; he has the power of statement, both for facts and for arguments; but far more serviceable than any of these gifts is his gift of preventing any one of them from running away with him. In other words, Mr. Bright seems to have, in a high degree, that very uncommon thing, common-sense.

I am aware that a charge frequently made against Mr. Bright by cold, timid, and conservative critics, is that he lacks precisely this balance of mental power. But it may be suspected whether, after all, this criticism does not come from people who themselves lack the very balance which they accuse him of wanting. Is it not legitimate to remind them that the warmth of emotion and the occasional vehemence of speech which Mr. Bright exhibits in the popular cause may, under the circumstances, be a proof of a well-regulated mind; and that their own insensibility to the moral force and the pathos of the popular claims, instead of indicating a philosophical nature, may rather mark an ill-developed and an ill-regulated one ? Unless philosophers are to be defined as human beings not allowed to keep a conscience or a heart, is it not true that the argument for the redress of a great wrong to human nature may at last become so urgent that even a philosopher shall have a right to employ Young's stern assurance:

> " On such a theme 't were impious to be calm;
> Passion is reason, transport temper here."

At all events, it is natural that politicians who are nearly frozen to death with social selfishness, or nearly frightened to death at the ominous advance of Liberalism, should look upon the democratic ardor, the faith in man, and the political courage of John Bright as madness; just as Coleridge's fellow-students at the university, who, carousing till two or three o'clock in the morning, voted him drunk, for the very excellent reason that, having been studying Greek all the evening instead of drinking champagne, he " looked so very queer."

A delightful chapter might be written on the humor of John Bright; and the gift of humor is one of his most effective weapons as an orator. It not only illumines and relieves the weightier passages of his speech, but it mows down prejudice and carries rout and dismay where serious argument would be simply swamped in dislike or in mere stupidity. Not even Disraeli can punish an opponent more severely; for the wit of Disraeli, though keener and more subtile, is absolutely without humor: it is neither so hearty as Bright's nor backed by so genial a power of reasoning. Mr. Bright's wit is thoroughly human; it is broad, spontaneous, and sympathetic; and even when it seizes its victim and binds him to the whipping-post, and lays on the lashes without ever counting them, it does so with a glee so genuine and so magnetic, that even the poor devil himself, who does keep account of the strokes, must nearly break into laughter in the midst of his own yells.

When, in the reform struggle of the last spring, Mr. Lowe and Mr. Horsman seceded from the Liberals, and began to put on the airs of leadership and to have much to say about their new party, John Bright made infinite fun of "this party of two," as he called it, by comparing it to a Scotch terrier, "which was so covered with hair that you could not tell which was the head and which the tail." The roars of mirth with which both sides of the House shook that night reverberated through the kingdom; and thenceforward for many months, at all the Liberal meetings somebody was seen, at the fitting time in the evening, to rouse again the merry shouts of the people by elevating upon the platform a huge print of this hirsute and bicephalous beast, lithographs of which were in demand in all parts of the island. It was in the same speech that Mr. Bright produced even greater effects, both in the House and in the country, by speaking of the bench on which the new party was sitting as " the cave of Adullam, where were to resort everyone that was in distress, and everyone that was in debt, and everyone that was discontented"; and thus the droll nickname of " Adullamites " was born into the vocabulary of English politics — a jest which did more service in checking treason to the Liberal cause than all the grave orations that had been made within a twelvemonth.

But Mr. Bright's humor, even when it does not manifest itself in these great epochal displays, — whereby a joke of his has sometimes changed the face of English politics and upset or confirmed a cabinet, — may be constantly observed dancing and rippling along the edge of all his utterances. Replying to a conservative speech of Bulwer-Lytton's last spring, he said :

" The right honorable baronet comes down once or twice during the session, and makes a speech which gives great satisfaction to the House, provided you do not pay the least attention to what there is in it. I mean, that in tone, manner, and imagery we are pleased; but I am grieved when I find to what side he gives his great influence. In his speech last night he used generous words of the workingmen, and told us how there was a tie, not only of interest but of respect and affection, between the rich and the laboring poor. But to give them compliments of this kind and flattery of this nature, and not votes, seems to me to be a thing which will go down very ill with the great body of the people, who are asking that at least some of them may be admitted to a representation in this House. It reminds me very much of a couplet, which I am sure the right honorable gentleman will remember, from Shenstone:

"He kicked them down-stairs with such a sweet grace,
They may think he is handing them up.'"

As an instance of the breadth and freedom of humor in which he sometimes allows himself to indulge, I may cite a passage from a great speech I heard him make in Birmingham last August—a passage which, as I well remember, stirred very effectually the most tumultuous mirth of his audience:

"The Government of Lord Derby in the House of Commons, sitting all in a row, reminds me of a number of amusing and ingenious gentlemen whom, I dare say, some of you have seen and listened to —Christy's minstrels. The Christy's minstrels, if

I am not misinformed, when they are clean washed are white men; but they come before the audience as black as the blackest negro, and by this transformation it is expected that their jokes and their songs will be more amusing to the audience. The Derby minstrels reverse this arrangement; they pretend to be liberal and white, but the fact is, if you come near them and examine them closely, you will find them to be just as black and curly as the Tories have ever been."

While listening to Mr. Bright, or while reading the newspaper reports of his speeches, I have been reminded of a description which Harington gives of the eloquence of one of his senators in "Oceana": "Never was there goose so stuck with lard as my Lord Epimonus's speech with laughter." Looking over the speeches that Mr. Bright made during a part of the time in which I have been accustomed to hear him, I will select, as further illustrations of his quiet humor and sarcasm, a few of those passages, which, like my Lord Epimonus's speeches, are "stuck with laughter." "The foundation for revolution in almost every country, unless history lies dreadfully, has been laid by those who pretended to be specially conservative." Referring to Mr. Disraeli's ambition for office, he said: "The right honorable gentleman has no doubt somewhere a parliamentary Bradshaw—all his lines converge to

Downing Street." On another occasion he remarked: "I sometimes fear that the House of Lords is no longer the Temple of Honor, the path to which lies through the Temple of Virtue. It has become too much a refuge for worn-out members of the House of Commons." In reply to the charge of repetition in his speeches, he said:

"I believe that a charge of this nature was brought more than two thousand years ago against one of the wisest of the ancients. They said that he was always saying the same thing about the same thing; and he asked them in return whether they expected him to say a different thing about the same thing. I have another answer to make to these critics, and it is this: When they have answered what I have already said about this thing, then I will try to tell them something new."

Speaking of the efforts to carry an election in Brecon, he said: "I hear from private sources that at least two noble families have been very active in their exertions—noble families that, I am told, came in with the Conqueror, and, as far as I know, it is the only thing that they ever did." Concerning the conduct of the rich toward the poor, he said:

"They are personally kind enough, but they don't care for the people in the bulk. They have read a passage in Holy Writ that 'the poor ye have always with you'; and therefore they imagine that it is a providential arrangement that a small section of the people should be rich and powerful, and that the great mass of the people should be hard-working and poor."

It is, then, impossible to form a just opinion of the quality and power of John Bright as an orator without taking into account the great part which humor plays in his discourse. By appointment of Providence, he is an iconoclast. He has always had, and he still has, rough and grim work to do. He is terribly in earnest. The most of what he says is deeply serious. He has been obliged to array against himself the hatred of the richest, and the opacity of the stupidest, classes in England. How valuable to such an orator, both for attack and for defence, for the enforcement of his logic, for the relief of his style, for the protection of his friends, for the vanquishment of his foes, in short, for all the cut-and-thrust business of a great oratorical guerilla in a stormy legislative assembly, is the possession of that ethereal gift which can send forward a jest to pave the way for a syllogism, which can bayonet a political ruffian with a joke, which can even compel a blockhead to blush at his own folly!

JOHN BRIGHT

V

AS AN ORATOR

THERE seems a sort of irony in that appointment by which such a man as John Bright was to find himself born among a sect distinguished by the tenets of meekness and non-resistance. In how facetious a mood Destiny must have been when it arranged that the most renowned of living Quakers should be the most pugnacious of living politicians! Appreciating to the full the English love of fair play, of pluck, manliness, and magnanimity, the hereditary follower of George Fox has the spirit of a knight-errant; he ranges over the field of politics as if for the very joy of combat, to rout monsters from their caves, and despots from their castles, breaking a lance with every defiant horseman, and eager to rescue all weak mortals that suffer under wrong. Jousts, skirmishes, battles, seem to be his native element. There are persons whose creeds are written upon their faces, and the catechism they swear by is recited in their gait. No one reads "Quaker" in the features or the bearing of John Bright. Of middle height, broad-shouldered, thick-set, with a smooth, expansive English face,—none the less English that it retains just a tinge of the national attribute of haughtiness,—with small, gray eyes, raying out a discriminative sort of kindness, before which folly, meanness, and insincerity must stand very uncomfortable; with a mouth compressed, imperious, and eloquent, and that kind of firm, strong, combative chin, which those men have of whom it is usually said that "they will not stand any nonsense,"—he moves upon his platform or confronts the Tory benches with an air rather more than resigned to any little disturbance that his intimate enemies may feel inclined to precipitate upon him. We do not suppose that Cobden fell behind Bright in saying severe things, not only of but to the privileged classes across the broad aisle of the House of Commons; but it was always evident that Cobden said these things reluctantly. It is quite possible that Mr. Bright feels a similar reluctance, but no one, from Mr. Bright's manner, would be likely to accuse him of it.

There is a story told of the two friends which illustrates this point of contrast between them. It is said that they were once driving down to the House of Commons together, upon occasion of a great debate in which they were to take part. Cobden, as usual before speaking, was anxious and depressed. Bright, on the contrary, was full of the "gaudium certaminis," anticipating the proud rapture of the coming fray and of their own inevitable victory.

"I know you can enjoy it all," said Cobden, "and perhaps it is best so. But I hate having to beard in this way hundreds of well-meaning, wrong-headed people, and to face the look of rage and loathing with which they regard me. I had a thousand times rather not have to do it; but it must be done."

I have directed attention to the extraordinary prominence of combativeness in Mr. Bright's nature, because it enables us to indicate an equally prominent quality in his oratory. That oratory, being the unaffected effluence of the man himself, is steeped through and through with this combative element. His sentences are braced up and muscular with the spirit of warfare. They are constituted of noble English; they are permeated by humor; they rear a very solid structure of fact and argument, but their form and hue and moving life are contributed by his combativeness. His rhetoric is the rhetoric of strife. The words of John Bright have the Luther-like ring; they are half-battles. Each sentence smites like the blow of an old warrior's axe. He seems to go into a speech as a ship-of-war does into action, clearing the decks and sending all non-combatants below. He has carried to perfection what William Wirt has referred to as " the feliciter audax, both in manner and expression." Kinglake, the historian, has wittily accounted for Mr. Bright's power as an aggressive orator by noting the inseparable connection between his heart and tongue: " Besides that he was honest and fearless; besides that, with a ringing voice, he had all the clearness and force that resulted from his one-sided method of thinking, he had the advantage of generally being able to speak in a state of sincere anger." It seems that Mr. Bright would largely sympathize with the idea of preaching held by John Knox, who used to refer to his successors in the ministry as " the faithful men that God of his mercie shall appoint to fight after me." It is a confirmation of what I have been saying that during Mr. Bright's whole career, early and late, the descriptions of his oratory one meets with commonly fall into the imagery of strife. Said the American, Henry Colman, twenty-one years ago:

" Bright is a sort of Quaker, plain-spoken, fearless, denunciatory, and excessively bitter, because he has been often baited both in and out of Parliament, and scents the hounds before they get upon his track; and so far from flying seems to delight in turning round and holding them at bay, occasionally stopping the yelping of a cur by the slap of his tail, or tossing a fierce mastiff upon his horns high in the air."

Said the Frenchman, Louis Blanc, not long ago: "John Bright's sentences sound to the charge, ringing like the blast of a bugle."

To state the impression which the rising of Mr. Bright in Parliament makes upon an observer, it would perhaps be accurate to say, under favor of the amiable gentlemen of the P. R., that he always looks as if he "meant business." The vast majority of speakers there do not so impress you. They appear to have risen to illustrate the bad acoustic qualities of the chamber, or to get a little elocutionary practice, or because they know that their constituents will be expecting a speech from them, or to obtain the proud satisfaction of seeing their names the next day in the "Times," or even, as a waggish member, Mr. John Hardy, lately confessed, "in pure self-defence, just as one is compelled to smoke on entering a room filled with smokers." Accordingly, in much of the speaking of the House of Commons there is an indirectness, an incertitude, a rambling and shambling method of getting to the point, even an indifference about ever getting there at all; a lack of positive conviction; an absence of earnestness; an abject loitering in commonplace, unredeemed even by the unctuous bluster, the innocent and jubilant rhodomontade, of an American Congressman; and finally, timidity—that last infirmity of ignoble minds—a timidity that cowers before the puerilities of conventionalism with an abasement deadening to every spark of original thought or feeling. Mr. Bright differs from most other speakers in the House of Commons just as a man with an animating and a grand purpose differs from a man without any particular purpose at all. This is indeed the tonic of his eloquence. Then, too, Mr. Bright early learned that whosoever in this world has anything worthy to do or to say must rid his soul of the fear of man—if, indeed, as in Mr. Bright's case seems unlikely, he ever had such a thing as the fear of man in his soul. Thus, with something to say, and with perfect courage to say it; with a sense of justice, a tenderness of heart, and an excitability that flame into insupportable indignation over wrong perpetrated by the strong; with an utterance grave, powerful, fluent; with a love of details in narrative or in statistical argument sufficient to give body to the aspiring soul of his eloquence; with an imagination kindling over his theme and giving to it both warmth and unity, yet saved by his logical sense and his humor from that fault of Curran's whereby " his flights of eloquence were commonly flights from the cause of his client"; with his theoretical notions of right tempered by a knowledge of the practical difficulties in the way of reducing these notions to reality; he is the master of a diction at once terse, copious, splendid, and effective; of an

> " Eloquence that charms and burns,
> Maddens, soothes, and wins by turns."

It is painful to be obliged to mention that though Mr. Bright is but fifty-five years of age, the physical power requisite to popular oratory is failing him. His mental conditions were never so perfect as now. He is fully ripe. His intellectual touch along the keys of expression is now firm, precise, full, confident. All his later utterances have those precious qualities which only years and the best fruition of years can give—breadth, solidity, compactness, a balanced and calm wisdom, the stormy enthusiasm of an earlier day mellowed by the generous lessons of sorrow. Now more than ever has Mr. Bright the spiritual fitness to be a great political teacher for England and the world. But the living voice is the only vehicle of expression he has ever employed, and his voice has lost its endurance. He seems to have a seated bronchial disease. The last time I heard him he spoke with an appearance of difficulty and pain. It was only by great moderation, by frequently pausing, and especially by soothing his throat with wine at almost every sentence, that he was able to get through at all. And this has been his experience of late.

At the great reform demonstration recently made in Manchester, Mr. T. B. Potter, the successor of Cobden, said of John Bright: " He can no longer be regarded as merely the member for Birmingham, but as the exponent of the will of a free people "; and, later in the same meeting, an address was presented to Mr. Bright in the name of the people of Lancashire, which contained these words:

"You will not return to Parliament simply as the representative of a single borough, but as the elected tribune of a mighty people. Face to face you have seen this people; you have a right to speak for the east and the west, the north and the south; when you are assailed with the taunts and jibes and sneers of a proud oligarchy, who use every weapon that slander and malice can suggest, we pray you to remember that a whole nation stands at your back, resolutely determined to support you while you battle for its liberties."

This it is, at last, which crowns the splendid energy of John Bright as an orator: it is that with all his resources of language, with all his superb endowments of humor, sarcasm, invective, logic, with all the contagion of his common-sense, with all the effects wrought by his directness of purpose, his fervor, his transparent honesty, his compassionateness, and especially by that courage of his which exults in the fierce transports of combat, he seems to stand forth in the House of Commons with a nation at his back. He is the oratorical vicar of the disfranchised majority. A strange resonance is thus given to his single voice. He speaks with a reduplicated majesty, because the stern cry of the unrepresented millions of Great Britain utters itself through his lips.

HER MAJESTY THE QUEEN

I

NOT the least of the many important services rendered by the departed Prince Consort to the royal family of England was that he taught them how to save their pennies. As the Emperor Augustus boasted that he found Rome a city of brick and left it a city of marble, so the late handsome, wise, and thrifty Albert might have boasted that he found the English royal family bankrupts and left them millionaires. All the boys of George the Third were beggars. George the Fourth, the most unblushing beggar of the lot, was always up to his eyes, if not quite over head, in debt. William the Fourth had many a time to depend on the generosity of one of his future subjects for a five-pound note. The Duke of Kent, the father of Queen Victoria, was more than once kept from positive want by borrowing money from the father of our own Robert Dale Owen; and, even just before the birth of

Victoria, the Duke had some difficulty in raising funds enough to pay his wife's travelling expenses from the continent back to England, in order that the expected heir to the throne might be born in the land which he, she, or it was to reign over. When, however, Prince Albert came from Saxe-Coburg, in 1840, and married the young Queen, he forthwith put a new face upon affairs. It is said that he recommended to his good wife the plan of laying up something for a rainy day, and that he even predicted a rainy day for royalty over all Europe before a great many years. He seems to have encouraged her in the economical habits that her excellent mother had already taught her—not even frowning when she took her morning walks in a calico-print dress—calico print, by the way, made by Richard Cobden. The Prince Consort appears also to have organized on an extended scale a system of retrenchment and reform in household expenses, as well as of prudence in the investment of their surplus funds. Indeed, so far was this practice of royal thrift carried that it became the theme of querulous complaint on the part of their loyal critics, who will sometimes tell you how Her Majesty and the late Prince used to huckster their onions and cabbage from their Windsor farm—as if such traffic were not, after all, a very royal privilege! For are we not assured by Montesquieu that even Charlemagne was accustomed to raise the wind now and then by selling the superfluous vegetables from his gardens, and the redundant eggs from the farmyards of his private domains?

The English people, whatever they may think, at any particular moment, of the person of royalty, are very proud of the office—as is proved by the fact of their paying for it so generously. They deal with their ruling family in no parsimonious spirit. The Prince himself, so soon as he arrived, was provided with a pleasant little income for his personal use. First of all, it was proposed in Parliament to settle upon him during life the sum of $250,000 a year; but Mr. Hume, a Scotch member, with a thoughtfulness in such matters characteristic of his side of the Tweed, objecting to this, and saying that he " did not see the use of setting a young man down in the streets of London with so much money in his pockets," the amount was reduced to $150,000 a year. In addition, the Prince had bestowed upon him a great number of lucrative offices, military and civil, about many of which the best thing was that, while they conferred considerable salaries, they did not imply the necessity of doing any work. Thus from all these sources, as well as from his model farm and from his other fortunate investments, it is estimated that the Prince must have saved, during the twenty-one years of his married life, not less than two millions of dollars. If to this you add Mr. Neeld's bequest of two and a half millions of dollars, you will discover that the royal family, though now bereaved of its head, must still be in tolerably comfortable circumstances; and this, too, before you have taken any account of the parliamentary appropriations and the other vast emoluments which the surviving members of the family have always enjoyed. Let us linger a moment over these cheerful items. And here I venture to caution my American readers, on their peril, that the annual allowance made to Her Majesty " for the support of her household and the dignity of her crown " is not to be described by any such democratic and vulgar word as " salary "; but that it is to be known by the more considerate phrase of " the civil list." It amounts to $1,925,000 per year, of which $300,000 per year go to Her Majesty's privy purse. We shall be aided in our efforts still further to appreciate the pecuniary magnanimity of our English cousins, if we take notice of the fact that, having thus provided for the support of Prince Albert and the Queen, it was also deemed right for the House of Commons to see to it that each successive child born of this happy and eminently prolific marriage, should also have an endowment, at the public expense, worthy of its princely station. I have before me now the blue book, containing the finance accounts of the British Empire as presented to the House of Commons in June, 1866; and I find therein the following list of annuities which the tax-payers of Great Britain had the privilege of providing during the previous year for those amiable and ornamental personages who constitute the royal family. It will be understood, of course, that I have changed the figures by translating them roughly into our own currency at the gold standard.

Trustees of the late Prince Leopold George	$50,000
Duchess of Cambridge	30,000
Princess Augusta	15,000
Duke of Cambridge	60,000
Princess Mary of Cambridge	15,000
Princess Royal (of Prussia)	40,000
Princess Alice	30,000
Prince of Wales	200,000
Princess of Wales	50,000
Prince Alfred	75,000
Princess Helena	30,000
Total	$595,000

It should be added that the Prince of Wales also enjoys the revenues of the Duchy of Cornwall, now amounting to about $250,000 per year; and that the Princess of Wales is to receive, in case of widowhood, a pension of $150,000 per year during life. Let it not be forgotten, also, that these great sums are raised by the English people in addition to the money they pay each year for the ordinary expenses of the government, including the salaries of the ministers of state, judges, and others, as well as the enormous cost of the army and navy!

"Sir," said a scion of the house of Austria, "the trade I live by is that of royalty." I think most readers will agree with me that in England at least this is one of the most profitable trades now going. The English pay every two years and a quarter into the private purses of their Queen and her family a sum of money about equal to the entire amount which the United States has paid to its chief magistrates from the first inauguration of Washington to the second inauguration of Lincoln! Does it not fill us at this moment with a sort of self-applausive content only to reflect that we Americans are clever enough to obtain even so choice a luxury as Andrew Johnson for about one thirty-fifth of the cost of Queen Victoria and her family!

II

Nearly all Americans who come to the immediate dominions of the Queen, carrying with them, as they are sure to do, the reverence for her and the affection which are so prevalent in our country, soon find themselves reminded, as they converse with loyal Britons, of the value of distance in lending enchantment to all mortal, especially to all royal, affairs.

It has seemed to me that the personal authority of Queen Victoria is, at present, more complete,—that is, more unbroken by any form of harsh criticism,—in those obstreperous communities across the Atlantic which some ninety years ago rose in rebellion against her grandfather, than it is in the very islands which then objected to our rebellion, and which still remain under the rather metaphorical sway of her sceptre. According to my observation, at least, it is far more common for Americans to speak, with unreserved love and homage, of the nobleness and of the womanly virtues of the English Queen, than it is for the English people themselves to do so.

Perhaps the difference between England and America, so far as Her Majesty is concerned, would be more accurately expressed by saying that, while among us there is but one opinion about her, among the English there seem to be not only two opinions but many. You will, indeed, find in England vast numbers of people who love the Queen with a devotion almost passing the right of any creature to receive; who are in a state of serene assurance that she is absolutely perfect; who regard the slightest breath of criticism breathed toward her as nothing short of blasphemy; who will recite for you, with evident emotion, Tennyson's lofty and loving song to her who is, in his heart as in theirs, indeed " revered, beloved!" I notice, however, that one does not meet so many of this class of undoubting devotees in London and in circles impinging upon the court, as in those less blasé portions of the realm where royalty is never or seldom seen, but where it still hovers over them, with all its poetic colors, as an awful and a sanctifying presence—as some beautiful mediæval myth.

If any of us think this devotion just a trifle overdone, we can but consider it as a picturesque and an amiable weakness, and pay to it the tribute of our silent respect. But, in reality, what we Americans have usually to complain of, is a propensity quite the reverse: it is the frequent disposition we encounter among the English people to wound our American loyalty to their Queen by saying about her all manner of censorious things which to us at first are startling by their unexpectedness, and which from first to last seem rather ignoble in their harshness and in their proximity to calumnious tattle and back-stairs gossip. And this disposition, so far as I can judge, is not limited to any particular class of the people. You will meet it on every round of the social ladder, from the tradesman to the duchess—expressed, I am told, the most fiercely on those rounds nearest the top. Nay, it is just now the cue of society in London—it is the shibboleth of those who would be thought particularly at home in the fashionable spheres—to shrug the shoulder and sneer at the personal faults and infirmities of Her Sacred Majesty. For an American now coming into the kingdom, it is just this that constitutes a painful paradox and a disenchantment. Of course, we are abundantly accustomed in America to the freeman's privilege of picking flaws in our Presidents, and we do it all the time, and with hearty vigor and good-will; but as to the Queen,—why, ever since we were born, we have heard of her only as the good wife, the good mother, the good ruler, and to us always the good friend; and it more than surprises us, it hurts us, to discover that among her own people she can be the subject of jibes, of sneers, even of rather disagreeable tittle-tattle.

I am not about to make my pen the conduit for any of this ungenerous gossip, but as an observer of whatever here is legitimately observable, I cannot refuse to report the fact of its existence. Neither do I know how to account for its origin, except by saying that it seems, in part at least, the outgrowth of the discontent of the metropolis over the dulness in society and the dulness in trade resulting from the Queen's long retirement from her capital. But if this chatter about the present monarch of England is without foundation in truth, as doubtless it is, we shall have to conclude that she is as cruelly maligned as almost any character in history. Certainly, her experience seems to furnish another illustration of that mournful picture of human nature given by the clerk of her council, Mr. Arthur Helps, who tells how falsehoods may be so often repeated that " calumny shall at last make a cloud appear like a mountain." It is true that all monarchs, however wise and good, like all public servants under other names, have been subject to these vicissitudes in the general opinion,—these ebbings and flowings of the tide of popularity. As to the Queen of England, whose faithful and benignant reign has extended almost to the close of its third decade, she seems just now to be at the ebb in the tide of popularity; but, surely, this can be nothing more than a temporary incident. So vast and so genuine are her claims upon the respect and love of her people, that it would require not much of an event, at any moment, to set the tide of popular affection flowing back again, with a mighty foam and roar, up to the very foot of her throne.

III

One can hardly help thinking that the Queen of England must be often bewildered at the strange incongruities in the loyalty of her people toward her. She is the burden of the first toast and of the last song in every assemblage in all her wide dominions; and, wherever she moves, she is saluted with marks of reverence which seem little short of adoration. A few years ago she walked on the sands of Kirkcaldy; and, as was most natural, she left there the print of her foot. Immediately the mark in the sand was measured, its length and breadth recorded, a cast taken of it and then solemnly deposited among the precious relics of the town. She was once embarking at Brighton. It had been forgotten to lay down the carpet which is usually placed between her carriage and her boat. The mayor and the aldermen at once plucked off their scarlet robes and cast them beneath her sacred feet, to walk upon. Yet, with all these extravagant demonstrations of homage, she can hardly fail to notice that, when the one day of all the year comes round which is set apart for her peculiar honor, only the shops of those tradesmen with whom she specially deals have any gas to spare for the illumination in her behalf. Everything in the land is spoken of as hers. It is Her Majesty's faithful Commons, Her Majesty's mails, Her Majesty's highways, Her Majesty's steamships, Her Majesty's army and navy. Yet everybody else knows, and she cannot help knowing, that all this is but a figure and a fiction—the shadow of a royal authority whose substance was torn away and annihilated in 1688. The navy is not hers: she cannot appoint or remove the smallest middy in all her fleets. The army is not hers: she cannot control the movements of one corporal's squad in all the ranks which swear allegiance to her name. Her steamships will carry her—on payment of the usual fare; her highways are open to her—as they are to the dirtiest peasant who stands gazing at her chariot; her mails will carry her letters—at the rate of one penny the half-ounce; and as to her faithful Commons —they would cause the whole island to quake with war and to run with blood before they would yield back to her one iota of all the authority which they fiercely wrested from her ancestors. She bears all the magnificent insignia of an absolute monarch; she retains all the ancient and awful titles of majesty; but there is left to her scarcely one solitary political function of regal power. As Mr. Grote has wittily expressed it, her office is " a remarkable combination of the fiction of superhuman grandeur and license with the reality of an invisible strait-waistcoat." In the British ship-of-state the monarch is neither the propelling force nor the steering one—she is merely ballast; and never before was ballast so sumptuously gilded, or so lavishly paid for!

There is something almost tragic in the fact that the ruler of an empire whose drum-beats pace in unbroken march quite round the world, should herself be denied a privilege which even the lowliest of her subjects possess—the privilege of grief. Twice or thrice every year the " Times " newspaper reads to her a lecture on the duty of conquering this sorrow for her husband. A chorus of complaint rises to her from all quarters and from every class on account of the stagnation in social and commercial life which her retirement occasions. Shopkeepers fail in business; and forthwith in the bankruptcy court they lay the blame on the Queen. It is curious that nearly two hundred years ago the English people were finding fault with another English monarch, for the same crime of sorrow; and Matthew Prior has left a little poem in which he expostulates with William the Third for giving way to mourning over the loss of Queen Mary:

> "If prest with grief our monarch droops,
> In vain the British lions roar."

That appears to be about the nature and the extent of the present calamity in England: the British lions cannot roar to as much purpose as usual. But surely every disinterested and humane person must insist that it is quite as important that British widows should be allowed to grieve as that British lions should continue to roar; and that, if these noble beasts do indeed find that they roar in vain, it might be just as well for them and for the world if they had the good sense to stop roaring altogether.

Queen Victoria began her reign with a splendor of popularity almost unparalleled in modern times. She is apparently ending it under sorrows that might well crush both heart and brain. "The throne," said Napoleon, in one of his democratic moods, "is merely a piece of wood covered with velvet." The Queen of England must have found very little velvet during these later years upon that chair of majesty. Rather must she have often realized the bitterness of the sarcasm of Juvenal, who spoke of the "heavy gew-gaw called a crown." Her own subjects have turned upon her with unkind criticisms so numerous that, like the cloud of arrows discharged by an army of Parthians, they shut out the sun.

The poet-laureate has sought to anticipate

the voice of the future concerning her reign, and he imagines that a portion of that verdict will be,

"God gave her peace."

It is a common opinion that the reign of Victoria has been a peaceful one; but the truth is, there has scarcely been a day since she ascended the throne that she has not had a war or two on her hands. There was the Canada war, the Syrian war, the Afghanistan war, the Scinde and Moultan war, two Punjaub wars, two Kaffir wars, the Assam war, the Burma war, three Chinese wars, the Persian war, the Russian war, the Japan war, unnumbered New Zealand wars, the Bhootan war, the wars internal to India and to Ceylon, the wars in West Africa and in South America. Henry Ward Beecher stated a truth, which is as applicable to the period of Victoria as it is to that of any of her predecessors, when, in Exeter Hall, in 1863, to an immense multitude of Englishmen, he said of England, "Her ensign symbolizes her history —the cross in a field of blood."

As we recall, however, that touching and beautiful prophecy of Tennyson's, we cannot refuse to cherish the hope that its other particulars may be more perfectly verified than the one which refers to the peacefulness of her reign:

" She wrought her people lasting good ;

Her court was pure ; her life serene ;
  God gave her peace ; her land reposed ;
  A thousand claims to reverence closed
In her as mother, wife, and queen ;

And statesmen at her council met
  Who knew the seasons, when to take
  Occasion by the hand, and make
The bounds of freedom wider yet,

By shaping some august decree
  Which kept her throne unshaken still,
  Broad-based upon her people's will,
And compassed by the inviolate sea."

London, 1866.

THE HOME AND GRAVE OF COLERIDGE

THE second Sunday that I passed in England—a dreamy, sweet May day in 1863—was spent by me in part with the Howitts at their cosey home in Highgate, perhaps the quaintest and most picturesque of the suburbs of London. I remember even now with what interest I mounted upon the top of the omnibus in the Tottenham Court Road, and passed forth through the vast brick wilderness of the town, towards the antique and still rural village where Whittington had sat down in despair, and had heard the far-off bells of Bow Church sing to him that immortal song of cockney magnificence:

" Turn again, Whittington, turn again, Whittington !
Thrice lord mayor of London " ;

and where also, for many centuries, beneath the pair of antlers kept at the inn, the burlesque oath that Byron speaks of had been administered to every newcomer, pledging him " never to drink weak ale—when he could get strong; never to kiss the maid—when he could kiss the mistress; never to take a bad thing—when he could get a better."

But it was not, I must own, of these associations of Highgate that I thought the most as our omnibus rumbled along over the stones towards the place. For, blending with the excitement of anticipating the acquaintance of two such celebrated and endeared writers as William and Mary Howitt, was the tender and reverent memory of Samuel Taylor Coleridge. I remembered that Highgate had been his place of refuge for the last twenty years of his life; and I thought how many hundreds of times along this same highway he must have trudged to and fro between his gentle asylum and the great city, and how many hundreds of pilgrims, too, of every civil land and language, had gone this way to listen to the marvellous monologues of the transcendent dreamer.

I had not been with the Howitts many minutes, when I spoke the name of Coleridge, and of my interest in being near his old haunts. At once the daughter, Miss Howitt, kindly offered to gratify my curiosity by taking me to the house where the poet used to live, which was but a little way from their own. We had to walk to the top of the hill on which Highgate stands, and from which—it being four hundred feet higher than the dome of St. Paul's—one looks off southward upon a delicious English landscape—waving parks, undulating meadows, hedges, and lordly mansions nearly lost in trees—and, still farther to the south, the awful city itself reposing like some sleeping monster, half buried in the clouds of its own breath.

A bend in the old road at the brow of Highgate Hill brought us within view of the wide calm street of the village, on the left of which, standing back a little way from its garden gate, was the plain, two-storied, brick house, for so many years occupied by Coleridge's loving protector, "Mr. Gillman, Surgeon." It is now a long time since the Gillmans have lived there; and at the time of my visit the house was empty and to be let. I wondered that a house with such a history could be without a tenant for a single day. Hundreds of the American students of English poetry and of English philosophy would be glad, I should suppose, to pay an extra rental for the aroma of fame and genius still clinging to those walls. William Howitt told me that an ardent American professor once tried to buy the door of the room which Coleridge used for his study. I confess that nothing but a very abject consideration prevented me from attempting to buy all the doors, and indeed the whole house with them, and packing them all off to America. There is a deep garden behind the house in which the poet used to walk; but his favorite place for open-air meditation and quiet exercise, was under the row of majestic elms which stretch away in the wide street from the front gate, and form a sort of unfenced park rather than a highway. Miss Howitt graciously endured my untravelled enthusiasm by accompanying me into the garden, and by procuring for me a view of the vacant rooms which had held the presence of Coleridge, and had reverberated with the incomparable music of his talk.

After staring at the house, and all about it, and all within it, as long as I dared to do, we wandered slowly under the great trees where the glorious sad man used to walk; and then, coming round by the old churchyard where his body lies buried, I contented myself for that time with a mere glance at the spot.

But three years later, in this November, 1866, I have carried out the purpose I had kept alive, of making a more deliberate pilgrimage to Coleridge's grave. I had seen in the papers that a chapel was then building in the churchyard, and that the graves of Coleridge and of his family were to be left untouched, in the middle of a crypt beneath the chapel. On arriving alone at the churchyard, I was unable to find the graves I sought. In reply to a question from me, the workmen on the new building stared at me curiously as a sentimental interloper; and all the more, when I made bold to ask them to show me the grave of Coleridge. They knew nothing about Coleridge or his grave; but said rather compassionately that there was an old man in the village, one Eagles, a seedsman, who had lived here always, and knew every live man, and the grave of every dead one—and doubtless he could tell me what I wanted to know. I strolled along the street till I came to Mr. Eagles's little shop; and opening the sleepy door, with its bell jangling a shrill outcry at my invasion, I found a quiet, tall, elderly man, standing behind a little counter, and busy with papers of seeds. His appearance was, indeed, refined, benignant, even venerable; and to my questions he replied promptly, and with none of the pomposity or of the obsequiousness so common to petty English tradesmen. He told me how to find the grave; and as I turned to go, thanking him, I merely added, "I come from a country a long way off—a country where Coleridge is greatly honored—from America." Upon this he turned upon me with a brightened face and a manner surprised into cordiality, exclaiming: "This is very extraordinary. I have had a great many American gentlemen here for the same errand, in former years, before the war; almost none for a long time now. I shall be most happy to go with you, and show you the place. I am going that way."

As we went, he told me what he could remember about Coleridge. As a boy he had often seen and talked with the famous man; and he showed me the very path under the trees where Coleridge used to walk, and he pointed out one tree before which he had seen the poet stop perfectly still for a long time, and stare into vacancy. As an apprentice to a gardener, Eagles used to work near Mr. Gillman's house, and had hundreds of times stopped to gaze at the aged man, with his long, flowing white locks, his great eyes, his kind, wise face, as he paced slowly up and down beneath these elms, with a book in hand. The tones of the poet's voice, Eagles said, were very rich, beautiful, and friendly; and he was a great favorite with all the little boys and girls of the village, who used to rush up to him affectionately and hold merry talks with him. I asked the gardener if he remembered seeing any of Coleridge's friends coming to visit him.

"Oh, yes," said he, "I used to see many great folks; but I did n't know who they were. But at the house of my master there lodged a literary gentleman—I forget his name; and one evening he gave a dinner in his room to Coleridge, and to Charles Lamb, and others. Yes, I remember well Charles Lamb—he was so queer-looking and he came very often. I was in the next room, and heard them when they got very merry over their wine. Coleridge's voice I heard most of the time. Some one gave the toast, ' Here's to the lasses!' and some one else shouted, ' With an offering of glasses!' and threw a large tray of them on the floor."

The kind man by this time had conducted me to the top of the steps leading into the unfinished crypt. With him I descended, and there saw the several coffins holding the mortal remains of the poet, his wife, his beloved daughter, and her husband. On one of these coffins I solemnly placed my hand. This was the coffin on which was written with black paint, " S. T. C., August, 1834." As I held my hand so close to that sacred dust, I thought of the pathetic lines which the poet had jotted down, as an epitaph for himself, but a few months before he died:

" Stop, Christian passer-by—stop, child of God,
  And read with gentle breast. Beneath this sod
  A poet lies, or that which once seemed he—
  Oh, lift one thought in prayer for S. T. C. ;
  That he who many a year with toil of breath
  Found death in life, may here find life in death.
  Mercy for praise—to be forgiven for fame
  He asked, and hoped, through Christ. Do thou the same."

10 November, 1866.

A SUNDAY IN WALES

AT the end of the week, not very long ago, I found myself in Cardiff, an ambitious little Welsh city, which, within the space of forty years, by the prophetic enterprise of the late Marquis of Bute in the enlargement of its docks, has been raised from a beggarly hamlet of feudal reminiscences to be a rich and growing mart with thirty thousand inhabitants. I was anxious, however, to pass the Sunday in an atmosphere of unmitigated Welsh; and Cardiff, I thought, resting on the rim of the sea, with the flags of all nations flying over its docks and the tongues of all nations chattering in its streets, had sunken all Cymric individuality in the complexities of a bustling seaport town,—that medley of wild, wanton, ravenous sea-monsters let loose upon land,—that Babel of uproar, dirt, and polyglot profanity,—that saddening hotch-potch of whatever flits or floats of the scum of nations. I resolved, with the morning light, to go inland a few miles, up among the mountains of Glamorganshire, and find a genuine Welsh village, hear a genuine Welsh sermon, eat a genuine Welsh dinner, and see what a genuine Welsh Sunday is like. I had the luck to pitch upon the name of Caerphilly. So to Caerphilly I went.

The train, which seemed half reluctant to disturb the drowsy quiet of Sunday morning along the valley of the Taff, yet tried to appease its conscience by carrying a few Methodist and Baptist exhorters and dropping them tenderly at their several preaching stations, reaching Caerphilly just as the more tardy villagers were straggling to their churches. Situated about half a mile from the station, in the midst of a vast circular valley, whose circumference is a coronet of kingly mountains, this quaint, irregular, and very ancient village of eight hundred inhabitants crouches beneath the ruins of the famous old Caerphilly castle, next to the royal castle at Windsor the largest in the kingdom, and now, in its decay, the most majestic, the most extensive, and the gloomiest of the remains of ancient English architecture. I remembered some lines in " The Norman Horseshoe " of Sir Walter Scott:

> " From Chepstow's towers, ere dawn of morn,
> Was heard afar the bugle horn,
> And forth, in banded pomp and pride,
> Stout Clare and fiery Neville ride.
> They swore their banners broad should gleam
> In crimson light on Rhymney's stream ;

They vowed Caerphilly's sod should feel
The Norman charger's spurning heel."

Before alighting from the train I had a glimpse of the immense, solemn walls of the old castle, of its mouldering battlements, of its huge towers, all standing in the grandeur of a mighty sorrow and calmly awaiting, age after age, the slow hostility of fate. Though eager at once to visit the stately, the unhumbled ruin, I saw that now was my only chance of being present at a service in Welsh and of hearing a specimen of that celebrated eloquence, the eloquence of the Welsh pulpit. I knew that the old castle would stay. I was not so sure that the sermon would. Dropping into a stream of villagers along the road and listening to the incessant click and rattle and bang of their Celtic words, I was told by a man to whom I addressed myself, that the best preacher in the place was he of the Baptists— a verdict of rare sectarian magnanimity, as my informant himself was going to another congregation. A brisk walk soon brought me to the Baptist chapel; and as I approached I was made aware that the work there had already begun in earnest. The two doors were open; a very fervent prayer was being uttered; and many of the congregation had risen and turned about in their pews, bowing their faces upon the pew backs. Several of them, who were not too far rapt in prayer to perceive a stranger standing in the vestibule, condescendingly peeped through their fingers at me, and then pointed to a seat.

The room was nearly square, with a lofty old pulpit at the end opposite the doors, and a gallery running around the other three sides. It was well filled in every part. The minister was a young Welshman, with thick black hair parted in the middle, with dark, massive, and tough features, and an intense expression. His voice was incisive and sharp. The hard Welsh words were hurled from his tongue like stones from a catapult. There were in him the Celtic fire and passion; the consciousness that, in the simple minds of his hearers, he was invested with a mysterious authority; an appearance of invincible earnestness and determination. I could easily accept him as a very likely young Druid—if, indeed, Druids were ever young.

The congregation seemed composed of plain country-people, shopkeepers, miners, farm-laborers; and one portion of them from first to last enchained my attention. Directly in front of the pulpit was a large square pew, capable of holding about thirty persons, obviously a place of eminent and solemn honor; and on this occasion it was filled with men, mostly old men, all of them apparently being the more advanced and redoubtable saints of the community, the veterans and senators of the spiritual host. The lesser saints and the average sinners were accommodated with subordinate sittings at the sides and back of the room, or were compactly stowed away in the gallery; but into this great central box, as into a sacred enclosure, had gone the " potent, grave, and reverend seniors " of the flock; and I found that their function in the exciting exercises of the service was an important and a picturesque one. Some of them were men of strange visage: they seemed a group of seventeenth-century puritans, confessors, and religious heroes; they had grim, iron, old faces, stiffened into preternatural rigidity by the awfulness of their Sabbath occupation, and by the two or three centuries of Sabbatic severity which they had evidently lived. Altogether, they had the air of men who fasted and prayed; who defied the world, the flesh, and the devil; who kept their eyes fixed on one supreme thing with a gaze to be distracted by no terror and by no fascination; who came into the world on purpose to be prophets, apostles, martyrs, and Baptist deacons.

All this time the prayer was going on. Not one word was intelligible to me, and I was left to give my whole attention to the strange tones of the preacher's voice, to the vocal structure and anatomy of his sentences. There was something weird and impressive in it all. His utterance did not flow, it broke forth in jets and gushes. Then, at every pause, a series of inarticulate guttural sounds issued from the midst of the great pew, and occasionally from other parts of the room. At last the audible character of the prayer underwent a sudden and a most startling change; it rose high above the already fervent level at which I had first heard it, into a sort of ecstasy; and then there followed the wildest and most electrical sounds I had ever listened to. The speaker's voice became transfused by a terrific enthusiasm; his impetuous words leapt forth in torrents; they were not a vulgar shriek, they were not a canting bellow; they were a real old magnificent Druidic chant, the sentences taking form in perfect rhythm, flowing and ending with a cadence so wild, so poetic, so mysterious, that it made the blood thrill in one's veins. The effect on the congregation was tremendous. From the depths of the great pew the responses heaved loud, swift, distinct, and impassioned; they were re-echoed all round the room, and even from the remote heights of the gallery; and when, at last, this devout ecstasy of prayer lapsed into sudden silence, the cries of "Amen," and of certain Welsh ejaculations, continued from all parts of the room for nearly a minute, like the lingering and passionate reverberations of the speaker's own voice, or as if the people would try to storm heaven with a love and a desire that could not give over the supplication.

In Cardiff, afterwards, I was told that this stage of vocal and emotional ecstasy is the necessary final act of all Welsh prayers in public, and, as I soon discovered for myself, the necessary climax of all the important passages in the sermon. For ages the people have been accustomed to it. They await its coming as the sibyl might have awaited the rushing descent of the god. Their fiery Celtic natures are inflamed and electrified by its magnetic delight. It is a tempestuous spiritual intoxication to them, a spasm of devout phrensy, a rhapsody of heart and of brain struggling toward the Highest in an agony of prayer and praise. The Welsh ministers themselves, from childhood accustomed to observe its manifestations, unconsciously cultivate the art of reaching this rapt, impassioned stage. They learn to work themselves up to it whenever they preach or pray, like the lions referred to by Montaigne as goading themselves into madness by the lashings of their own tails. Yet, concerning these Welsh preachers, I do not mean to imply anything affected or disingenuous in this habit of theirs; and I can testify that its manifestations are as far as possible from being repulsive.

Next came a hymn. It was abominably sung; nay, it was not sung. Through linkèd discord long drawn out, it was simply twanged; the venerable patriarchs in the large pew, more especially, employing their big, ancient, sonorous noses as if they thought them originally constructed by the Creator for speaking-trumpets and organ-pipes, and that to contravene this divine ordination would have been impious.

At last came the sermon. The preacher began in a low, almost inaudible tone. His manner was so quiet and so informal that I supposed he was " giving out the notices." Soon, however, his words became more clear, his tones more earnest; and this fact was immediately signalized by the responses of the assemblage. Thus he proceeded for about ten minutes, gradually swinging into his theme and warming with his thought, accompanied at every step by the audible sympathy of his audience, until finally he seemed to reach the vantage-ground from which to bound forth into what I have indicated as the ecstatic stage. Now came once more those strange wild notes, that hurricane of oratorical rapture, those indescribably impassioned and rhythmic sentences which I have spoken of as concluding his prayer, only that in the sermon these were borne onward with greater freedom both of gesticulation on his part and of bodily movement on the part of his audience. In this torrent of Celtic eloquence he stopped as abruptly as before, and then began the next article of his sermon in the same quiet tones. This process of storm and calm was repeated, though at shorter intervals, five times in the course of his address. I have never in any other religious assemblage observed such excitement as was manifested in this little rustic congregation. Moreover, long before the conclusion of the service, I saw what efficient allies the preacher had in the venerable lay senators of the big front pew. Their devout and even sepulchral mien cast a sort of subduing shadow over the whole assembly. Their heads were the first to nod and sway in confirmation of the preacher's statements; their voices led the ceaseless rumble and shout in response to almost every sentence that fell from his lips. Those hard, iron faces became molten, and they gleamed with enthusiasm. The first notes of the hymn rose from the very midst of their sacred enclosure. They seemed to be, in look and in speech, in act and in attitude, the coryphæi and exemplars of devotion.

The sermon lasted but thirty minutes. In it all, I had been able to recognize only four words—Jericho, Jerusalem, Christmas Evans; but I am bound to confess that it was one of the most interesting, exciting, and profitable sermons I have ever listened to. Finally, the foregoing account is, I believe, a fair description of the general spirit and method of worship in the dissenting congregations of Wales.

I dare not here venture upon a history of the Welsh dinner which I got after the Welsh sermon, or of the magnificent ruins I visited after the Welsh dinner. Later in the day, in a delightful walk of several miles down the noble valley, I was struck with the general external observance of Sunday by all classes of the inhabitants. I encountered many groups of people, all in their decent Sunday garbs; and the little children whom I met, saluted the passing stranger with quaint marks of respect, which, to one accustomed to the pranks of London urchins, were almost embarrassing. I also saw along my route multitudes of placards posted against walls and pillars, and nearly all of these were the advertisements of quack doctors tendering their compassionate and confidential assistance to persons of both sexes who might be suffering the penalties of imprudence. In lonely rural scenes, amid the quietude of Sunday observances and the footfalls of returning worshippers, these saffron and parti-colored proclamations had an ominous significance: they recalled, even if they did not exactly confirm, the stinging epigram of the royal health-commissioners, that Wales is more addicted both to sermonizing and to sexual irregularity than any other part of the kingdom—always excepting Scotland!

January, 1866.

A PEEP AT THE CARDIFF CONSULATE

I HAVE lately seen a strange and touching sight. Having finished my pilgrimage to the places of chiefest interest in South Wales, the venerable cathedral of Llandaff, the vast ruins of Caerphilly, and the grand old feudal castle of Cardiff,—the latter still moaning with reminiscences of the cruelty of William Rufus and Henry I.,—I found several hours still left to me before the departure of the train. At such times, amid sights and sounds all alien and unfamiliar, the heart of the traveller is sure to throb with thoughts of home, and with that deep, slow ache of the soul which can be appeased only by something that comes from home. It occurred to me that the most homelike thing in this little city must be the American consulate. Accordingly, though personally unknown to Mr. Burch, the present incumbent of the office, I made sure of a courteous reception; and through the torrents of rain I tramped down the long, dirty, dismal street which borders the famous Bute docks; and far out near the pier-head, among the commercial representatives of all nations which use iron, burn coal, and send ships to sea, I found the building,—one floor of which is occupied as the American consular office. I blessed the man who invented consulates. With what joy, with what pride, with what a soothing sense of restfulness, does the American, long wandering in distant lands, find himself once more under the folds of the Flag Beautiful, and within the four walls even of some dingy office where yet his eyes moisten and swim at the sight of an old map of his country, of engravings of Washington and Lincoln, of a few rusty law-books with those homelike titles on their backs, and perhaps frowning over the bookcase a bust of Webster, looking a very " black Daniel " indeed, beneath the strata of official dust that has settled upon him in the course of several presidential administrations.

I had been guided to the right house by seeing a crowd of men and women, who appeared to be of the humblest class, standing in clusters in front of the building, patiently waiting in all the rain, earnestly talking in low tones, and ever and anon pointing up to the windows of the consulate. The passage and the stairs were thronged by them—some going up, some coming down, but all having the same intent, serious, burdened look. As I reached the door, it was sharply closed against a little company of these poor people, who sadly turned away, and, talking in low, anxious tones, walked downstairs. My own knock brought the clerk abruptly to the door, with a stern expression on his face as if he intended to turn me away too, but which relaxed into an invitation to enter as he discovered that possibly I might be on other business than my predecessors. Mr. Burch happened not to be within, but was expected every moment; and I accepted the polite intimation that I might await his coming. I had hardly got seated when there was another knock at the door; and they who came had hardly been turned away when there was still another knock, and another, and so on in rapid succession. What could it all mean? The clerk informed me that two weeks before they had given away a few copies of an official document relating to government assistance in emigrating to the United States. These documents, it seems, had flown like the winds among the poor working-people, both Irish and Welsh, throughout all this region; they had been carried back into the country, among the glens of the mountains, and down into the coal-pits and the iron-mines; they had been eagerly read by the furnace-fires, by the flickering lantern of the collier, by the blaze of peat on the cottager's hearth—they had lighted up hope in thousands of heavy hearts eagerly clutching at the dim possibility of escaping from their hard lot here to the wonderful land of promise beyond the sea. Immediately a stream of resolute aspirants began pouring into the consulate. Mr. Burch had intended merely to obtain the names of any who would like to go to America on particular conditions, and to report the probable number to the government; but the names came faster than he could take them, and it was necessary, in a few days, to announce that he could receive no more. But this announcement went on slow legs, and was quite unable to head off the glad tidings which were already rushing abroad; and every day since then had brought a repetition of the scene which I have just beheld. From many miles inland, and far along the coast, these poor creatures come to Cardiff. Unabashed by adverse rumors, they find their way to the American consulate; and there they stand in the street for hours together, in all weathers, till one after another they have actually gone to the consul's door and heard with their own ears the fatal answer.

Mr. Burch, who soon came in and gave me a very civil greeting, said that within the two preceding weeks there must have been two thousand personal applications at his door for passage to America; that this number could have been more than doubled had he held out the least encouragement; and that, if the government or a private company saw fit to undertake the matter, several thousand valuable laborers, experienced colliers, miners, and mechanics, would be glad to grasp at any arrangement by which they could get across the sea.

It was indeed saddening to watch the crowd below and listen to the incessant entreaties at the door. If any of us went to the window, straightway all faces were upturned, their eyes peering into ours with an inquiring and beseeching look, as if somehow in that room and in our persons their destiny resided, and the brightness and cheer of their future lives. There they stood—strong men and women, some of them with babes in arm—the rain coming down upon them heavy but unnoticed, gazing up at the windows and trying to glean from them some tokens of promise. Then the reiterated formula at the door between the clerk and the applicants was something as follows:

"We have called, please, sir, to put our names down, sir, in the book, sir, for America."

"We can't take any more names at present."

"But, sir, please do take ours, sir; we do wish to go, sir."

"I tell you we can't take any more names."

"But, sir, we 've come a long way."

"Sorry for it—can't take you" (partly closing the door).

"But, sir, tell us when we shall come again to see."

"Can't tell you now, you must go away;" and upon this the door roughly closed, and the poor candidates for expatriation would go down, looking very forlorn, and report the answer to their equally forlorn companions. In sheer self-defence it was necessary to treat them harshly.

I do not think any American could have stood where I stood, and have seen what I saw, without having his heart filled with sadness and compassion, and without feeling a nobler pride than ever in the name and mission of his country. Several times of late have I sat in the House of Commons, and, hearing from the lips of England's greatest statesmen glowing compliments for America, eloquent recognitions of her military greatness, her wealth of territory, and her political success, felt my joy and pride too great for silence. It was hard not to get up and shock the decorum of the whole assemblage by one huge Homeric shout: "I too am an American!" But it seemed to me to-day, as I stood at the windows of the consulate, or listened to the importunities at the door, that these poor peasants were paying a higher compliment and bearing a nobler testimony than was ever borne by the most affluent orator in Parliament. It did not nourish a boastful patriotic vanity; it was no food for national gasconade and assumption; it was a thought grander than the remembrance of our invincible citizen soldiery, of our boundless material resources; it was the simple and the sacred fact that to millions in all lands who are humble and heavy-laden this word AMERICA means all that is meant by the word HOPE. These poor, sad-faced creatures, standing before the American consulate in Cardiff, seemed to symbolize the struggling masses of all the populations of Europe, their weary fight with life's hardships, their toil which returns them just enough to let them keep on toiling, their rudeness and ignorance, their unthrift, their unhappiness, and their universal looking to that star which has risen in the west, and which, they think, shines not for peers, and for princes, and for taskmasters, but for men and women. And this is not a thought to build up the pyramid of national arrogance and conceit. Nay, it will rather bring tenderness to the heart and humility and tearful consecration.

It is an awful thing to have Providence put into a nation's hand that banner bearing only the word " Man." Dare we suffer that banner ever again to trail in the mire and hide from all eyes the one great word which God's own finger wrote upon it, and which gives to it a consecration infinitely more precious than any selfish inscription about race, or color, or class ?

It is an awful thing to be wholly trusted even by one human being; how much more so to be the object of the mysterious faith of millions. To these humble millions gazing over the sea, it is no fiction, it is no tinsel trick of rhetoric, that America is the star of humanity risen and shining in the west. But, though they do not know it, and might not appreciate it if told, there are still some evil vapors obscuring the shining of that star. It shines not yet with the full brightness with which it will gladden the earth, when they who live in its immediate light understand and accept the reason for its shining at all.

22 January, 1866.

ENGLISH PLUCK

PARTLY from an instinctive skepticism, partly also from a sort of whimsical rebound of combativeness, the most of us, probably, are apt to put a query over against any proposition which happens to be frequently and rather vauntingly asserted. It may be on some such principle that many persons, especially before coming to England, have their own private doubts about this thing renowned in all the four quarters of the earth as " English pluck." Of course no man, though born at the antipodes, who has even skimmed over the history of human affairs for the last thousand years, can doubt that the English are brave; but so are many other people—the French, the Spanish, the Austrians, for example—yet who ever hears of French pluck, or Spanish pluck, or Austrian pluck? The question is, whether there is in Englishmen any such pre-eminence and predominance in respect to this peculiar quality of physical fortitude, as to justify the celebrity it has attained in all the civilized languages of mankind.

I am not sure that I can give a satisfactory account of the subject; but I have some observations to make concerning it, which may at least assist the reflections of others.

Whether or not the English actually have more pluck than other races, it seems to me certain that they have more admiration for pluck; and that the incessant expression, age after age, of this genuine and passionate sentiment, may go far to account for the currency of the phrase which describes it. This national tendency to love and to laud the virtue of courage, finds its voice not merely in the poetry, the ethics, and the eloquence of England, but even in its vices and crimes, in its social manners, and in its traditional aphorisms of political and personal feeling.

There is an important sense in which all crime is cowardice; yet English crime certainly has less of the cowardly element than we find elsewhere. Even the magistrates set to punish crime in England have not always been able to withhold their admiration for some admirable traits of the thing they had to suppress—as the chief justice in Edward the Fourth's time, who rather boasted of the bold and manly qualities which then distinguished English highwaymen. There has always been plenty of murder done in these islands; but, commonly, it is not murder of the stealthy and subtle, that is, sneaking and dastardly, kind. English ruffians can hack and mangle to perfection; they can equal anybody in slashing and slaughter—in out-and-out horrid, bloody, and comprehensive butchery; but for finesse in killing, for velvet-footed, creeping, catlike, artistic " taking off," for letting out human souls through neatly executed apertures in the human body, for graceful, noiseless, clean murders, for deaths done scientifically with cloaked dagger and the exquisite poison, you must go—elsewhere! Let it be known, then, for the edification of whom it may concern, that the trade of murder in England is practised after the plucky type. It may be pleasant for you to reflect that if you come to England you will stand a fair chance of getting murdered in some other way than in the contemptible, insidious South-European or Oriental fashion.

The same characteristic of rough physical hardihood stamps itself upon the baser sports of England. Prize-fighting is objectionable enough; but in the quality of courage, how vastly removed from bull-fighting, that dastardly pastime of the tropics! Tom Sayers, mangled, blinded, streaming with blood, yet keeping on his legs and wagging his broken arm to receive the crushing blows of Heenan's twin battering-rams, with nothing left in him but his dogged pertinacity in pain, displayed exactly the quality which fixed like adamant the British lines at Waterloo. The strongest point in the defense of the ring in England, to-day, is the pretense that it is a seminary of courage; and probably all that is needed to eradicate the popularity of pugilism, is the repetition for a few more times of the spectacle presented the other day by Mace and Goss— the spectacle of two pugilists turned into two puppies.

Through the whole web of English politics you may trace the same thread of English pluck—a valor scorning the refinements of Macchiavelli, too proud to win by mere adroitness, marching to square-fronted defeat with a bluff and defiant joy. The resolution of the childless Highland mother in the old Jacobite song,

> "I ance had sons, but now hae nane,
> I bred them toiling sairly :
> And I wad bear them a' again
> And lose them a' for Chairlie,"

but gives the key-note to that noble, sturdy refrain of devotion unto death and of courage conquering despair, whose echoes resound through many centuries of English history.

It is an old political maxim that " Englishmen hate coalitions "—a maxim expressive of that unbending fortitude of nature which will neither strike flag to an enemy nor strike hands with him.

We come upon the same great quality in this people's character by following that strangely significant path which is beaten out for us across the wilderness of words. When a man has something to say, but does not dare to say it, and skulks into an ambiguity, or hides behind the corner of a verbal evasion, how do we commonly drive him forth ? " Sir, the English of your statement is "—so and so! Thus into the very texture of our daily speech is woven the conviction that a thing which is not honest, straightforward, fair and square, is not English. Who needs to be told that the corner-stone of such a character is that courage which rests on the moral side of what we understand by pluck ?

The fact which we are considering gives us a clue as to one cause of the gruff and crusty bearing of an Englishman. The verdict as to manners has gone against him in the great court of public opinion. When a stranger comes to him, his ways at first are undemonstrative and chilling; and when he goes among strangers he contrives to make himself the most unpopular of tourists. I do not deny that there is a fault here, and that there are other causes which conspire to produce it; I merely point out that this fault is largely the offspring of a virtue. He is brave enough to encounter your dislike. He is too courageous to lie to you by a pretense of cordiality before he really feels it. His pluck will not suffer him to bid for your approbation by skin-deep smiles, when he thinks the situation demands growls. Doubtless, extreme affability often lives next-door-neighbor to moral cowardice, and sometimes even in the same house.

I have been struck, both in English history and in English common life, with the grim, hard style of language with which they often dispose of bodily suffering. After Marston Moor, Oliver Cromwell wrote to his friend Valentine as follows: " Sir, God hath taken away your eldest son by a cannon-shot. It brake his leg. We were necessitated to have it cut off, whereof he died." There you get the tough fact itself without sentimental palaver or whimper. The popular ballads of England are eminently realistic in their allusions to murder. Theodore Hook has precisely caught their spirit in his horrible rhymed tale of the assassination of Mr. Henry Weare:

>" They cut his throat from ear to ear ;
> His skull they battered in ;
> His name was Mister Henry Weare—
> He lived at Lyon's inn."

Not many years ago a pious old Scotchman had a son, who went to college, who learned to wag his pow in a pulpit, who finally became a missionary. After some time a friend of the family, meeting the old man, inquired after the welfare of the missionary, and got only this answer: " The haithens ate him." What a fine old Englishman was he, who, at the siege of Exeter in 1549, brought out all his provisions to the famishing inhabitants, saying that " as he communicated to them all his store, so he would participate in all their wants, and that, for his part, before he would consent to yield up the city, he would feed on one arm and fight with the other."

There would be a considerable advantage if the whole English people were reduced to one man, that we might illustrate all its peculiarities by a single example. I do not know but that such a reduction was really made in the last century, and that old Dr. Johnson was the result. Was he not the one concentrated and quintessential Briton of all ages ? Does he not condense into his single individuality the most notable traits of the English race—its intellectual and moral energies, its superstitions, its rooted prejudices, its magnificent aspirations, its generosity, its overbearing harshness, its central tenderness within a husk of savagery ? And how worthily the grand old fellow stands for the quality of English pluck! One night, being attacked in the street by four men to whom he would not yield, he kept them all at bay until the watch came up, and carried both him and them to the round-house. In the theatre at Litchfield, Johnson having for a moment quitted a chair which was placed for him between the side scenes, a fellow-countryman took possession of it, and when Johnson on his return politely asked for his seat, rudely refused to give it up; whereupon Johnson laid hold of it and tossed both man and chair into the pit. Foote, the comedian, had resolved to imitate Johnson on the stage. Johnson went to Tom Davies, the bookseller, and asked him what was the common price of an oak stick, and being answered sixpence, " Why then, sir," said he, " give me leave to send your servant to purchase me a shilling one. I 'll have a double quantity; for I am told Foote means to take me off, as he calls it, and I am determined the fellow shall not do it with impunity." Foote heard of the purchase and —changed his programme.

During my residence in England I have taken great interest in observing in boys' schools the manifestation of this cardinal attribute of the Anglo-Saxon race. These establishments may or may not spend too much time over the accomplishment of manufacturing Greek iambics and of translating the language of Chatham into the language of Cicero; but they certainly breed manliness. The best thing which an English schoolboy learns from his fellows is courage, with its attendant virtues—respect for truth, and scorn of sneaks. Nowhere else is greater homage paid to pluck. Not long ago, I happened to be at a boys' school near London during the play-hour. A little fellow was brought in with a severe contusion of the forehead, from a stone. The blood was running freely down his face, but not one tear. He disdained even to appear personally concerned in the affair. In these schools, as I am told, if a boy who is holding a bat, flinches at the approach of the cricket-ball, he is " put into Coventry "—a punishment more terrific to him than the Pope's curse with bell, book, and candle. For a particular number of days he is simply ignored by every other boy in the school. No one will speak to him, look at him, walk with him, sit with him, help him, or make any reference to him. He is banished to the solitude of his own cowardice. He is made to feel to the core of his heart and to the marrow of all his two hundred and twenty-five bones, that death itself is vastly preferable to dodging. Few boys get " put into Coventry " a second time. The head master of a boys' school near Bath told me many facts to show

how the tone in such communities is all for Spartan grimness and for unflinching endurance and even silence under bodily pain. One day a boy got a deep gash in his arm from the spike of an iron fence; he fainted away and had to be carried into the house. Presently the surgeon began to operate on the boy, who neither winced nor groaned. "I never saw such a stoic," whispered the doctor; "I'm hurting him awfully." The master replied in a whisper, "It's owing to the other boys being here." As soon as the boys went out, the little patient began to roar with pain. "I'll stop this," said the master, and called back some of the boys to hold the wounded arm while the operation continued. The moment they appeared, the sufferer brushed off his tears with his other arm, and was as grimly silent as ever. The taunt of cowardice from the lips of the other boys,—for that he cared more than the hurt of the surgeon's knife. In "Tom Brown's School Days at Rugby" is this remark:

"It's very odd how almost all English boys love danger. You can get ten to join a game, or climb a tree, or swim a stream, where there's a chance of breaking their limbs, or getting drowned, for one who'll stay on level ground, or in his depth, or play quoits and bowls."

These little fellows cannot at all understand

how any boy can be such a muff as voluntarily to take a hand in any species of exercise which contains no good arrangement for smashing their heads, or fracturing a collar-bone, now and then.

We shall perhaps be less astonished at this worship of pluck in the nineteenth century, if we recall the fact that ever since the first century, when Tacitus spoke of it, physical hardihood has been cherished and honored among this people beyond almost every other virtue. Why should we wonder that, in our time, British schoolboys pay such homage to pluck, if, even in the time of Solinus, the first food given by the British mother to her new-born babe was meant to nourish in him scorn of danger and pain:

"When a woman is delivered of a male child, she lays its first food upon her husband's sword, and with the point gently puts it within the little one's mouth, praying to her country's deities that his death may in like manner be in the midst of arms."

1864.

POPULAR LECTURING

DICKENS and Thackeray made the golden discovery, some years ago, that the American lecture-platform is an uncommonly nice place for famous English authors to stand upon for a time—our people, apparently, being rather eager to atone to such authors for our piracy of their books, by crowding the lecture-rooms and the purses of such of that defrauded fraternity as will venture over the sea and give us a fair chance to see them and hear them. Unless all signs fail, this pleasant find is likely in our time to lead to many another sentimental journey from the eastern hemisphere into the western.

They manage these things differently in England. If I could paint but a tolerable sketch of English notions and modes in relation to popular lecturing, it would furnish no slight surprise to the most of us; and it would do much to explain—if indeed it be worth explaining—why Englishmen are more likely to come to America to lecture, than Americans are to go to England for that purpose.

One thing, of course, is absolutely necessary to the success of the lecture-system in any country, namely, that first-rate men should consent to furnish the lectures. Surely by this time nothing ought to be plainer to our much-enduring race, than that first-rate lectures can never, by any contrivance, be got out of second-rate men; and without first-rate lectures, the system of having any lectures at all collapses into a farce. It becomes, then, a question of literary statesmanship, how to attract to this field the services of able and brilliant men. At the outset, it is desirable that the profession of lecturing should be one at least of some social consideration. This, however, is a condition which can be supplied, provided that the other terms are met; for the access to any honest calling of men of high character and of shining talent would soon shame from it the skin-deep curse of conventional inferiority. In the next place, the profession must offer such pecuniary inducements as to tempt men of the highest order of talent to give to it their deliberate attention. In the third place, it must, by its absolute freedom from all trammels upon thought and utterance, present a field of earnest practical influence.

By a very odd conspiracy of unfortunate circumstances, it has happened that each of these three conditions is wanting in England, and that, in consequence, the English lecture-system, inaugurated by Lord Brougham, and by other great personages, nearly half a century ago, in the midst of proud and gladdening omens, has turned out a rather ridiculous failure.

I

When, some ten or fifteen years since, several literary men in England began to show a disposition to imitate here the audacious example of Thackeray, by delivering popular lectures for pay, the London journals came forth with denunciations of the whole proceeding, and declared that for a distinguished author thus to make a public exhibition of himself for money was beneath his dignity both as a literary man and as a gentleman.

This idea may be a strange one to us; but to Englishmen it is not in the least so. It is the most natural deduction from the English philosophy of gentility. That philosophy scarcely recognizes anything as really genteel if done for pay. Thus, Englishmen would think it ineffably vulgar if their members of Parliament, like our Congressmen, were to receive a salary for their services. Even paid authorship savors rather too much of the shop to suit the taste of the highest dabblers in authorship;

accordingly Lord Derby keeps himself from the common herd of book-makers by devoting to a public object the profits of his translation of Homer. James Prior mentions that in the best circles of London he used to hear it urged against Edmund Burke, that in early life that great man was so abject as to receive compensation for his literary labors. It is related by Lord Lytton of himself, that when for the first time he became a candidate for Parliament, the following charge was alleged against him in order to prove that he could not be of a good family—" Why, Mr. Bulwer is an author!" English ideas of gentility have grown up, in the course of ages, in the presence of a magnificent hereditary aristocracy, whose enormous possessions enable its members to be independent of pecuniary compensation for anything they choose to do. To take pay for anything, is to confess your poverty; and to do that, is to confess the unpardonable sin. " In other countries," says Lord Lytton, in the pleasant book in which he gives the incident just mentioned, " poverty is a misfortune; with us it is a crime." " The want of fortune," exclaimed Lord Nelson, " is a crime which I can never get over."

It is, indeed, difficult to understand why the paid writers who conduct the London journals should have become so alarmed at the other paid writers who wanted to conduct the public lectures,—except that the latter business, as matters stand in England, is felt to be a few degrees more ignominious than the former, since it is a more immediate and a more personal exposure of one's need of earning money by the sweat of his brain.

They make a wide distinction in England between occasionally lecturing for nothing, and regularly lecturing for a fee. The one is an act of patronage; the other is an act of professional service. And this pretty distinction is by no means one of recent birth. That it existed even in Addison's time appears from the laughable account in the "Spectator" of the stage-struck country-gentleman who acted the part of the lion at the theatre, and who afterward said in his defense that he did it gratuitously!

I remember a story bearing upon the point, in connection with the distinguished lecturer, Mrs. Clara Lucas Balfour,—for, by the way, the invention of lady-lecturers is an honor not belonging to ourselves. While Lucy Stone was still playing with doll-babies, before Anna Dickinson was born, Mrs. Balfour had already begun to entrance English audiences with an oratory so brilliant, so refined, and so commanding, as to conquer, at least for herself, some exemption from English antipathy to female eloquence. An English lady of high social position was relating to me one day the romantic story of Mrs. Balfour's early career; how, being born of a somewhat distinguished family, she married below her station; how she was repudiated by her nearest relatives; how she resolutely entered the profession of lecturing, and won by it both livelihood and distinction. I innocently remarked that Mrs. Balfour's friends, in pride at her success, must have long since lost their resentment at her marriage. "Oh, dear me, no!" was the fervent reply; "for, you know, lecturing is so low!"

Perhaps there is nothing else among American customs more bewildering to the English people than that some of our most renowned and dignified statesmen, like Charles Sumner and Schuyler Colfax, are in the habit of lecturing for money. It is true that Lord Brougham and Lord Carlisle used to go down occasionally to the mechanics' institutes and deliver lectures; but every man, woman, and child in England knew that it was without the slightest pecuniary return, and was indeed an affair of aristocratic condescension. Lord Shaftesbury, Disraeli, Gladstone, Bright, sometimes do the same; but no committee would any more think of offering money to them for a lecture, than an old Hebrew prophet would have tendered shekels to the archangel Gabriel for the favor of an apocalyptic visit. There is a characteristic anecdote connected with this subject, preserved of that ferocious antagonist of aristocracy, William Cobbett. He had been on a lecturing tour through Scotland, and had publicly announced that in the very next season he would return to Scotland for a similar purpose. Before the next season, however, he was elected to Parliament; whereupon he threw up his Scottish engagements. On being called to account for so doing, he frankly replied that he " thought lecturing would be very undignified for a member of Parliament." One of the ablest and noblest of the radical members now in the House of Commons once told me that, after making his maiden speech there, many years ago, he involuntarily overheard in the lobby two members talking about him. " Who is this —— ? " " Oh," was the reply, accompanied by a sneer appropriate to the utterance of so blasting an indictment, " he 's an old anti-corn-law lecturer." " It is very true," remarked this noble radical to me, after relating the story, " it is very true that I did lecture against the corn laws; but then I never took a penny in my life for doing it ! " Though a radical, he was a good Englishman still !

II

Such being the bad eminence of professional lecturing in England, it is not likely that able and sensitively organized men, with the pick of the professions before them, would choose this vocation in preference to others of a more assured dignity; unless, indeed, they were impelled to it by an overwhelming sense of peculiar fitness, or by the strong expectation of special advantages as regards remuneration and usefulness. I imagine, for example, that the two most eminent professional lecturers in the kingdom, George Dawson and Henry Vincent, one of whom is an acute thinker and a scholar of considerable attainments, and both of whom possess extraordinary personal force, must have been conscious of special aptitudes for this form of work; for surely the fees which, on the English system, are usually given to lecturers, can have presented to them no very seductive bait. Hawthorne has a passage of solemn fun in which he speculates concerning the bewilderment which must assail an Englishman after death, on reaching a world where the institution of dinner is left out of the daily programme. It has seemed to me that our English cousins would be quite as much puzzled to find themselves arrived in a world where society is no longer divided into upper, middle, and lower classes; for, whatever may be the caste distinctions which prevail just over the cloudy border, we may venture to assume that they are not exactly adjusted to the English basis.

One immense difference between the lecture-system of America and that of England is that, while ours is designed for all the people, theirs is framed for only a small fragment of the people, to wit, for the more prosperous working-men, and for the retail tradesmen.

When, just half a century ago, England began to repose after her long death-struggle with Napoleon, she reposed on a very uncomfortable couch: bankruptcy, riot, famine, political discontent, and the grim ferocity of religious discord, all presided over by an idiot king, and by a regent who was at once a dandy, a drunkard, a coward, and a rake. In the midst of this gloom, brave men and women groped and struggled towards the popular relief through every conceivable method of amelioration. Then it was that poets and statesmen and philosophers and divines put their heads together in order to invent some engine against the ignorance which rested like a black vapor along the lower slopes of society. One result of these noble plottings was the organization of the Society for the Diffusion of Knowledge; and another was the establishment of mechanics' institutes. It was the intention of the latter, by the means of class-instruction and of lectures, to popularize knowledge by night for poor men and women who had to work by day; and an essential feature of the original scheme was, that the lectures should be given by persons able to talk wisely and attractively, and willing to do so for nothing.

The plan took like a strong contagion. All abroad in the land, in England and in Scotland, in Wales, in Ireland, it rushed and fructified. In an incredibly short time there were hundreds of mechanics' institutes in the kingdom. Of course, this swift development of an infinite demand for popular lectures transcended the resources of gratuitous supply. It was all very pleasant to lecture for five or six times; but country clergymen, already with a sufficiently obstinate cure of souls on their hands, and mild gentlemen in easy circumstances, and noble lords with a turn for philanthropy, could hardly be expected to keep up this sort of thing all winter, and year after year, tossed about on dreary journeys of doubtful utility, and kept awake five or six nights a week only to make their fellow-creatures very sleepy. It became necessary, in order to keep the lectures agoing, that the institutes should offer such small pay, say a guinea or two per night, as would be an inducement to schoolmasters on short allowance, to dissenting ministers trying hard to keep soul and body together, to young barristers waiting for briefs, and to others of that sort. Gradually the lectures expanded into a wider range of topics, into general literature and the ethics of society. A few really bright and able men, like the two whom I lately named, entered the field in the hope of doing and of getting good. But it was not a calling to get rich in. The institutes, made up of mechanics and shopkeepers, were never afflicted with plethora in the treasury department. They had to fix the price of admission to the lectures at an extremely low rate; and the fee which could be paid to the lecturer necessarily corresponded with the price to be given by the hearer. The precious attribute of our American system of lectures is, that they are for the American people at large, and not for any particular fragment of the American people. But over England still rests the ineradicable reminiscence of feudalism. The English people live and move and have their being in upper classes, middle classes, and lower classes. Never, except in some rare and imperial agitation of the general mind, can it be said of the English nation, that, like Wordsworth's cloud, " it moveth altogether, if it move at all." The system of popular lectures, begun for the benefit of the humbler classes, continues for their benefit; and the gentry and the aristocracy, whose participation would elevate it in dignity and efficiency, keep aloof from its privileges as carefully as they would from the privileges of the poorhouse. Lecturing, therefore, being the luxury of the poor, gets paid for at their price; that price obviously being such as to command those only who are willing to part with their oratory for a remarkably slight consideration.

According to my estimate, the average fee for a lecture in the English institutes is three guineas. There are scores of men in the field who lecture for two guineas, for one guinea, for half a guinea; while a certain blissful minority are rewarded for their efforts by the appalling sum of four, five, six, or even seven guineas. To add to our appreciation of the financial charms of popular lecturing in England, it should be mentioned that out of the above lavish rewards the lecturer is usually expected to pay his own travelling expenses and hotel bills.

I have before me now two official documents, one American, the other English, each giving a list of the professional lecturers and of the fees charged by them in their respective countries. A few extracts from these documents will intensify the statements I have just made concerning the paltriness of English lecture fees, by contrast with the generous rates which prevail in America.

Taking the American document first, I have classified its names according to the fees, beginning with the highest.

$500—Professor Agassiz.
$200—Charles Sumner, John B. Gough.
$150—Henry Vincent, Anna Dickinson.
$125-150—Theodore Tilton, Wendell Phillips.
$80-110-150—Prof. E. L. Youmans.
$100-120—C. Oscanyan.
$110—Rev. G. H. Hepworth.
$85-110—E. P. Whipple.
$100—Dr. Holland, Rev. F. Vinton, D.D.; Henry C. Deming, Geo. Vandenhoff, Rev. W. H. Milburn, J. C. Burrows, Josiah Quincy, Dr. Hayes, Colonel T. W. Higginson, Professor Tripp, Charles A. Slack, George Sumner, Frederick Douglass.
$80-100—G. A. Townsend, B. F. Taylor, A. G. Laurie.
$75-100—Prof. M. T. Brown, Clara Barton, Grace Greenwood, Major Merwin, H. L. Reade.
$88.40—Josh Billings.
$75—Prof. A. J. Upson, John Lord, Rev. J. W. Bailey, Miner Griswold, Dio Lewis.
$60-75—Rev. John S. C. Abbott, Rev. J. C. Fletcher.
$50-75—J. F. Manning, Mrs. Hazlett, George W. Bungay, Dr. R. K. Browne.
$60—E. M. Booth.

The names of at least five eminent lecturers do not occur in the above list: Henry Ward Beecher, who never lectures for less than $200; Dr. Chapin and George William Curtis, who probably receive $150; Mr. Emerson, who, I suppose, is usually paid a little less; and Mr. Colfax, whose terms are at least $200.

The English document is a catalogue of lecturers, issued by the celebrated Society of Arts. In this circular the lecturers are divided into two classes, the paid and the unpaid; the latter including two hundred and thirty-five names, and the former two hundred and sixty-six.

In glancing over this array of two hundred and thirty-five kind gentlemen who thus proffer their eloquence to the public at no other cost to the said public than its willingness to hear them, one soon discovers that the most of them are clergymen in country towns, physicians, lawyers, and retired army officers; while the rest are without titles which indicate their positions in the world. One thing in this list is a little singular,—the paucity of names with a reputation strong enough to have crossed the Atlantic. Almost the only distinguished name is that of J. Payne Collier. No doubt these gratuitous lecturers are very amiable persons; and I can testify from personal knowledge that several of them are very bright and pleasing lecturers. Still, it must be confessed that upon this list, as a whole, there falls the fatal shadow of that law of nature which compels everything in the universe to get its just price. Do these gentlemen get theirs? I recall two things which seem to menace an affirmative answer: one is an axiom tossed about among the English institutes, that they cannot afford to engage the gratuitous lecturers; and the other is a witticism of Gottfried Kinkel, the German poet and lecturer, now an exile in England, who, one day turning over this very pamphlet and running his eye down these long columns of unpaid lecturers, said to me: " There, you see what competition we have in all these fine fellows who are anxious to lecture for nothing. Yet perhaps the competition is n't so great after all —they probably charge exactly what they are worth."

But we are more particularly interested in the list of paid lecturers; and to that we turn for a moment. The beginning of this list bears no slight resemblance to the beginning of the human race:

" Adam, W., Matlock, Derbyshire.
" Terms: For one lecture, two guineas ; for two three guineas."

The next gentleman whom we observe is somewhat more aspiring in his demands:

"Anderson, John Corbet, author and artist, 2 Portland Place, Croydon.

"Terms: The two lectures for five guineas, if delivered within twelve miles of London; beyond that distance, expenses also."

The scale continues to rise:

"Applebee, J. K., Handsworth, Birmingham.

"Terms: Five guineas per lecture. A proportionate reduction for two or more lectures. Institutions newly established, or with limited means, favorably considered."

"Balfour, Mrs. Clara Lucas, Reigate, Surrey.

"Terms: Five guineas a lecture, subject to occasional deduction to small or struggling institutions."

The next lecturer is a little indefinite, but modest:

"Baxter, William R., Cotham Place, Bristol.

"Terms: A small fee, according to previous arrangement."

Presently we come upon an illustrious name:

"Blanc, Louis, 14 Merton-road, South Kensington.

"Terms: £10."

Fifty dollars for a lecture from this splendid man would, in America, be but a trifling fee; but in England it is so far beyond the means of the institutes as to cause his exclusion from their platforms.

Here, also, is a distinguished name:

"Buckland, Frank T., Regent's Park Barracks.
"Terms: £5."

Nothing could be finer or more reasonable than the attitude of the gentleman whose name here follows:

"Burns, Rev. Dawson, 335 Strand, W. C.
"Where institutions can afford to pay, the Rev. Dawson Burns charges in proportion to ability; where not, might gratuitously assist, if not far distant from London."

"Burr, T. W., F.R.A.S., F.C.S., etc., 12 Paternoster Row, London.
"Mr. Burr is always open to entertain favorably any application to lecture on payment of expenses, where assistance is fairly required."

"Burton, John, 27 Great Russell Street, London.
"Terms: According to circumstances."

"Busk, Captain Hans, United University Club, S. W.
"Captain Busk originally lectured gratuitously, but the demands upon his time were so great, and the costs incurred for travelling expenses were so heavy, that he was compelled to decline engagements where no remuneration was offered."

And served them right, Captain Busk!

"Craig, John, F.E.I.S., Glasgow.

"Terms: Two guineas for one lecture; but if the funds of an institution are low, on expenses being paid, the fee will be nominal."

The next gentleman, it appears, has a fancy for lecturing on the Greek tragedians.

"Davies, Rev. Charles Maurice, M.A., 72 Queen's Road, Bayswater, W.

"Terms: According to funds of institution. No objections to lecture gratuitously to institutions needing help, if they can furnish their own chorus."

Ah, but there's the rub!

Here we rest, near the beginning of the letter D. The remainder of the catalogue presents no new characteristics, while that which we have gone over abundantly illustrates the extent of the pecuniary attractions offered to professional lecturing in England. The results of this system of beggarly fees are simply fatal to the lecture-system here. A curse of pettiness shrivels the whole scheme. In contrast with the magnanimity of the American system, everything is lean, scant, miserly. With here and there an exception, only fourth- to tenth-rate men pay any attention to the business. Were the rewards of lecturing what they might be, and what in any community resting on a basis of social catholicism they would be—were they, in short, proportioned to the gains of thorough and brilliant exertion in the other cerebral professions, it would not be long before able scholars, authors, journalists, preachers, and publicists would be attracted to this valiant and forceful calling; the participation in it of such men would give to the whole at once dignity, scope, and perpetuity; and another engine for educating the public mind, and for creating public opinion, would be within the grasp of beneficent men, and would be wielded for the enlightenment, the elevation, and the happiness of the English people.

III

The degradation of the English lecture-system is carried still lower by the very causes which have brought it so low. If, even while conducted on so stingy a method, it were belittled by no stupid maxims about restricted discussion; if, even though it could not give large fees, it would give free platforms; if, in the absence of money, it had the presence of earnestness; if, while unable to tempt by pecuniary attractions, it did tempt by the attractions of a fair field for real exertion on the great, pulse-possessing themes of the day, it would still be a system deserving of respect for itself, and it would be capable of securing the services of men who had some respect for themselves. There would be dignity even in its indigence.

But such is not at all the case. The ultimate weakness and shame of the English lecture-system are portrayed in one word, neutrality—about the most contemptible word in the English language. It invites men to come to its platforms and to discourse there upon all subjects except those which men are the most interested in,—those vast fascinating problems of political and religious thought on which the quick spirit of these times is moving. The lecturer in the mechanics' institute is expected to stand in the most uncouth attitude possible for a man—his face averted from the age in which he lives! Or, should he presume to front squarely his own age, he must do so with a squint which observes only those matters of art, literature, biography, travel, social customs, which nobody cares enough about to quarrel over. I remember a lecturer at one of the best institutes of England, who had occasion to touch upon a literary aspect of the free-trade battle in England; but so sensitive were the audience to the impudence of this man in even verging upon a recent political topic, that they warned him off the territory in blunt, honest English fashion, by loud cries of "Shut up!" So, for the sake of peace in their lecture-system, they accept intellectual death!

It needs not many words to show how such an attempt at putting up barriers against free speech destroys all vitality, earnestness, power, manliness, in whatsoever involves the play of the human brain. The first touch of the fetter smites it with paralysis. Longinus says, "Only freemen are eloquent." In that instant when a man is told that he may not say what he will, the best life dies within him. Girdle your orchard-trees and look for fruit, sooner than expect eloquence or power to come out of any brain girdled with restrictions. And only in perfect freedom for the speaker can there be sustained interest for the hearer. There is nothing else to equal the charm of free political reference. This was one secret of the incomparable splendor of the Athenian drama and of its omnipotent influence over the Athenian people; it kept up every night a running fire of wit, wisdom, raillery, and invective upon the politics which had been going on during the day. Philosophy, art, history, mythology, were rescued from the ineffable curse of dryness by the dropping of that sweet dew that gathers only upon the brow of the Present.

Now is the solitary point of supreme interest for us. The past is dead; the future is unborn: this present is all that lives! Would you banish popular discussion from that one oasis of real existence in all the desert of time? And as it is folly to banish popular discussion from the present, so is it folly to banish it to the present. There should be no banishment at all, except of the word banishment. The platform should say to the man who stands on it: " Plant yourself upon me for your hour, and utter your thought! You are free! Give to these benches not what they think, but what you think! Draw your theme from what region you will—from past, present, or future, from earth, from heaven, or hell! Only let it be yours!"

Moreover, it is part of the disaster of any other method of conducting lectures, that it must disgust from the field exactly the men who are most needed in it. The great man will not stand it to be told what he shall or shall not say.

" In your country," said to me the other day a distinguished Englishman who has himself lectured with brilliant effect both in America and in England, "it is worthy of an honest man to lecture. The thing is honored as it deserves to be. Your platforms are free ; and a man can stand on them and keep his self-respect. He can say all that is in his heart. Your lecturers are not gagged; and a man feels that to talk in that free way to the people is to be about the real business of life. This cursed neutrality does n't belong on the American platform; and I hope to all the gods it 'll never get there. But in this country it 's totally different. They look upon lecturers as mountebanks and performers. It is a mere amusement, like negro minstrelsy. A lecturer is only a troupe of one; and if he is impudent enough to say anything in earnest about living questions, the people open their eyes and stare, with a sort of contemptuous incredulity, just as if the clown in the circus had undertaken to teach philosophy, or the harlequin in the pantomime had presumed to have any ideas upon statesmanship. No, sir, it 's a disgrace in England to lecture. Lecturing is mere tumbling."

At last, the people themselves, perceiving, with the swift scent of an intuition, that the man who talks to them is a man who can be made to succumb to their cries of " Shut up!" that he is therefore a second-rate man at best, that he has something worse than the best food to feed them with, lose straightway their respect for the lecturer, for themselves, and for the system which brought him and them together; and because living men, especially when sad with ten hours of toil, cannot muster up much appetite for the sapless shavings pared off from the dead trunk of the past, or even for art, or for philosophy, or for poetry, or for geology, or for what-not, if divorced from the throbbing political and religious interests which belong to the present, they soon come to loathe what are called instructive lectures, and they clamor for musicians and buffoons.

To this has the system of popular lectures fallen in England,—a system invented and put into operation by wise and benignant men, half a century ago, in full faith that it was to be a glorious instrument for the culture and the happiness of the English people.

1866.

ON CERTAIN ENGLISH HALLUCINATIONS TOUCHING AMERICA

THE longer I remain in England, the more perfectly do I seem to enter into the experience of a certain veracious countryman of mine—a New Englander and a son of Harvard—who, being in London so long ago as in the reign of Queen Anne, was much refreshed by the following bit of international talk held by him with a charming Englishwoman whom he met here in very excellent company:

"She asked me if all the people of my country were white, as she saw I was. She thought we were all black, as she supposed the Indians to be. She asked me how long I had been in the kingdom. When I told her 'a few months,' she said she was surprised to think how I could learn their language in so short a time. 'Methinks,' said she, 'you speak as plain English as I do.'"

Unfortunately, this traveller does not go on to mention any observations that fell from his fair English friend on the vast and bewildering theme of American geography; but had he done so, that single conversation, I doubt not, would have illustrated the three principal eccentricities of opinion which I refer to in the title of this paper, and which are still to be met with, not so infrequently, among our dear cousins over here:—First, that we Americans are black, certainly not white; secondly, that our ordinary speech is not English,—as, indeed, sometimes, perhaps it is not; and thirdly, that the topography of our country is one of those branches of knowledge which English people may sufficiently acquire by a process of evolution from their inward consciousness, and without the vulgar routine of studying mere maps or descriptive accounts of America. As to the continued existence of these curiosities of English opinion touching us and our country, I would merely add that I have myself stumbled upon a considerable amount of testimony relating thereto—testimony flowing on and on, in unbroken stream, all the way from the time of the good Queen Anne, down to the time of the good Queen Victoria.

I

As I have begun these remarks by referring to the state of things in the last century, it may be worth considering whether herein is not to be found the deeper clue to the origin of that unlucky quarrel which broke out between the English and the Americans about a hundred years ago,—a quarrel which already has had several notable consequences on both sides of the Atlantic, and is quite likely to have several more before the play is out. Can it be supposed, for instance, that if King George the Third had taken the trouble to become even tolerably well informed concerning his American subjects and their country, he would ever have blundered into the preposterous and disastrous policy he tried to enforce upon them? As to our side of the quarrel, also, is it not possible that, even back of our political suspicion and alarm over that policy, there lay a quite appreciable amount of offended pride—of American sensitiveness wounded, of provincial self-importance ruffled—merely through this persistent indifference of the mother country to even the most rudimental facts about us? Were we, then, such insignificant atoms in the great British Empire? Perhaps we could have managed to put up with the stamp act and the tea tax; but how were we ever to endure it that our English masters should deem us of so little account, that the knowledge neither of ourselves, nor of our history, nor of our geography, was worth the trouble of being correctly arrived at by them ?

Certainly, as one may easily find by dipping into the correspondence of the period, the mutterings of American discontent on this burning theme, preceded by many years those provoked by the several measures of George Grenville, Charles Townshend, and Lord North. Indeed, during all the repose of the colonies under the first two Georges, it was no uncommon thing for an American who had been in England to return to his own province laden with droll anecdotes to show the extremely hazy conceptions held by our English rulers concerning all American persons and things; and the laughter with which such tales would be told and listened to was often, perhaps, but a disguise for some inward bitterness over the unmistakable contempt for us thus revealed. When, for example, in the time of the Seven Years' War, the importance of defending Annapolis, in Nova Scotia, was suggested to George the Second's prime minister, the Duke of Newcastle, he replied, " Oh, yes, to be sure! Annapolis should be defended—Annapolis must be defended! By the way, where is Annapolis ? " Another token of this great man's equipment as a ruler of the British Empire was shown in the surprise he expressed on hearing that Cape Breton was actually an island. In 1755, just after the direful fiasco of General Braddock in the woods of Western Pennsylvania,—a fiasco due almost wholly to the fact that this brave Briton had not thought it worth his while to become even moderately well acquainted with the country through which he was to march his army, or with the ways of the people against whom he was going to fight,—a sarcastic comment on that British mode of doing business in America was made by a very able man in Maryland, a barrister who had received his education at Eton, at Cambridge, and at the Temple.

"Perhaps," said he jocosely, "in less than a century the Ministers of our gracious King may know that we inhabit a vast continent; and even the rural gentry over there will hear that we are not all black—that we live in houses, speak English, wear clothes, and have some faint notions of Christianity. 'Have you any cows or horses in Maryland, sir?' is a question I have been often asked, and when I answered in the affirmative, the reply has been, 'Oh, oh, you do not get them from old England, then?' But it is no wonder that such a question should be asked twenty miles from London, when a certain parliamentary committee, during the application for the salt bill, were wise enough to ask an American witness, 'Have you any rivers in America?' 'Ah, pray, how many?'

'Well, pray tell us, did you ever kill any fish in passing any of your rivers, as you call them?'"

No reader of " The Virginians "—a carefully studied historic picture of this very period of the Braddock fiasco—will fail to recall, as bearing upon our present discussion, the remark of Sir Miles Harrington to his young nephew, just arrived from Virginia:

"Thou hast a great look of thy father," said the jolly baronet. " Lord bless us, how we used to beat each other! Take it he was henpecked when he married, and Madam Esmond took the spirit out of him when she got him in her island. Virginia is an island. Ain't it an island?"

So, too, the official correspondence of certian Anglican prelates with their missionaries in America during those good old days, reveals in the ecclesiastical mind a similar state of unconcern as to all such pedantries as mere facts concerning those regions remote and infidel. Even in the early years of the reign of George the Third, the Archbishop of Canterbury, in writing to an eminent clergyman at New York, was accustomed to ask questions or to send directions touching missionaries in Newfoundland or in Georgia, His Grace supposing that those provinces were so near to New York that his correspondent would be in constant neighborly communication with the persons referred to. Amidst the earliest growls of discontent on the part of James Otis, over the new taxing policy of the government, one can even now detect the undertone of colonial annoyance on account of the very small place which we and our country then held in the British scheme of useful knowledge. "Divers of these colonies," exclaims that fiery agitator, "are well settled, not as the common people of England imagine, with a mongrel mixture of English, Indian, and negro, but with free-born British white subjects"; and he adds the facetious tale of a great minister of state, in the previous reign, who, "without knowing whether Jamaica lay in the Mediterranean, the Baltic, or the Moon," used to send thither official letters addressed "To the Governor of the Island of New England." Only a few months before the fight at Lexington, Colonel Barré told an American politician who was on a visit to London, that "more than two thirds of the people of England then supposed that the Americans were all negroes." Throughout the long war that followed, some of the Loyalists, during their enforced residence in England, found the sadness of their exile rather bitterly enlivened by the discovery of the extremely slight amount of information which the mother country had then cared to accumulate concerning themselves or the far-off land for which they then so passionately longed; and it is by no means strange that they occasionally divulged this discovery in forms verging close upon satire. For example, not long after the outbreak of hostilities between England and France in consequence of the help given by the latter to the Americans, there was reported in a Loyalist newspaper a droll conversation said to have taken place between the lord mayor of some provincial city and a friend of his, one " Sir Anthony K——g." " Good-day to you, my Lord," says Sir Anthony, meeting His Lordship in the street; " do but tell us the news." Lord Mayor: " Why, upon my conscience, there is great news!—the French have taken Umbrage." Sir Anthony: " Upon my soul, but I am very sorry to hear it. Are you sure it is true ?" Lord Mayor: " Very sure, for I heard it with my own ears: the secretary was just telling a gentleman that the French had certainly taken Umbrage." Sir Anthony: " Pray, my Lord, is Umbrage a strong place? Whereabouts does it lie ?" Lord Mayor: " Devil burn me, if I know; but it 's somewhere near Naples." Whereupon the two friends proceed to a neighboring book-shop to look into a gazetteer; but the bookseller himself is so clever as to be able to tell them offhand that " Umbrage is situated on the Po, and had indeed often before been taken by the French." Thus, it may be, the only apology the Loyalists could frame for British inattention to knowledge concerning America, lay in the quite palpable fact of British inattention, at that time, to knowledge concerning nearly all mundane countries and peoples outside the rim of their own islands.

II

Such, then, was the state of the British mind concerning us a hundred years ago. Very naturally, an American coming to England in these latter days, and remembering, perhaps, some such tales as these, is apt to suppose that, by the present time at least, a great change must have taken place, and that there can no longer exist here, to any extent, the mental condition out of which could be born such eccentric notions concerning us and our country. Nevertheless, before a very long stay here, he will be likely to find himself now and then rubbing his eyes in much bewilderment, and trying to make out whether he be really awake, or only dreaming that he hears some of the marvellous things that seem to be spoken to him. Only a few weeks ago, in the south of England, on my stating, in reply to a common inquiry, that I was from New England, my interrogator, a well-dressed and well-spoken person, immediately asked me whether New England was one of the Northern or one of the Southern States. On another occasion, when, in reply to the same question, I mentioned that immediately before coming over I had lived in Boston, the lady with whom I talked expressed her gratification at hearing this, since she hoped that, on my return, I would convey a message to her cousin who " lived near there, in New Orleans." When I gently explained to her that it might be a good while before I should be able to visit New Orleans, which was " a long way from Boston —nearly so far as Constantinople from London," she confessed that she had not imagined such a distance between the two towns, and " in fact, had supposed that they were near enough to be connected by omnibus."

I cannot tell how many times I have had the experience in railway carriages, hotels, and other public places, of arguing with intelligent men and women about the war then in progress in America, and of finding them display an altogether charming uncertainty as to whether the State of Ohio might border upon the Gulf of Mexico or the Gulf of St. Lawrence, whether the Potomac do not take its rise in the Rocky Mountains, and whether those same Rocky Mountains be not a series of ambitious protuberances somewhere in the vicinity of Vermont. While the war was going on, many a time have I amused myself by mildly requesting people who had their minds quite firmly made up that separation between the North and the South was the easiest and most natural thing in the world, to be so good as to indicate just where the line of separation should be drawn. I once made this request of a very agreeable gentleman who held a clerkship in a government office; and he instantly replied, with the sweet composure of one whose wisdom could be expected to receive no further illumination on this side of the grave, that, " for the purpose of a dividing line between the Northern and the Southern States, the most obvious geographical object would be the Mississippi River." In 1863, an eminent American clergyman just then in London told me of his dining with a distinguished company but an evening or two before, and of there getting into the usual discussion with his next neighbor at the table, who happened to be a member of Parliament. From this British statesman the American traveller then received a perfect flood of illumination as to the naturalness, and, indeed, the necessity, of a dismemberment of the Union.

"Why, there are you Northerners," said he,

"placed in North America all by yourselves! Then, there comes the isthmus—see, Panama, or whatever it is. Then, separated from you by this narrow bit of land, are the Southerners down there in South America. Now, my dear sir, I think you must admit, it is perfectly obvious that nature never meant you to be a Union!"

The reverend gentleman was forced to admit that something was, indeed, very obvious, and, in short, that he had never before been accustomed to view the problem in just that light.

Some time before the close of the war, I knew an English clergyman to maintain, in the presence of a full drawing-room, that " in this American war they ought to give their sympathy to the Virginians, because Virginia was originally settled by the Pilgrim Fathers, the most heroic stock that went out of England." Not long since, at a hotel in Wales, I met an affable gentleman who, not having then discovered that I was from America, very kindly gave me a vast amount of choice information about that country. Among other recondite things of his which I have stored away in my memory, was this,—that " the whole trouble in America is due to the fact that the country was originally settled, about the middle of the last century, by a great pack of spirit-rappers who ran away from England to avoid being roasted at the stake, as they should have been." I have found educated people here who have the idea that the civilized portion of the United States is a narrow strip of semi-luminous culture somewhere along the Atlantic coast; and that you have but to penetrate a few miles inland in order to reach the realms of primeval nature, and to encounter all the wild beasts of the forest. An English university man, much given to hunting in wild regions, once consulted me about an intended visit of his for such a purpose to New York, and he asked me " how far out of the town he would need to go in order to find good kangaroo shooting." From that moment, I have not wondered at the famous passage in Cobden's last speech, in which he expressed the wish to endow at Oxford and Cambridge a professorship of American history and geography: " I will undertake to say, and I speak advisedly, that I will take any undergraduate now at Oxford and Cambridge and ask him to put his finger on Chicago, and that he does not go within a thousand miles of it."

For my part, I hope not to be accused of pressing this subject in any unreasonable way. Of course, the minor details of a distant topography and history are not to be expected of any people, save, perhaps, among their specialists in such matters. Accordingly, as I think, Fenimore Cooper was hardly justifiable in his great astonishment at the venal infirmity of the late Lord Holland, who mentioned to Cooper that Lady Holland owned some land in America, " situated on the Genesee River in Connecticut." Perhaps, also, it would be equally unfair for us to make comment on a somewhat similar infirmity revealed by Mr. James Hannay, now the editor of " The Pall Mall Gazette," who stated in his " Life and Genius of Edgar Allan Poe," that his hero " was a native of Virginia," having been " born in Baltimore in 1811." These, I admit, are petty details, which, as regards a country so far off as America, it is perhaps absurd for us to think that our English kinsmen should be familiar with. After all, the truth seems to be, that knowledge of those portions of this planet which lie outside the boundaries of the United Kingdom have never yet been a matter to engage the very determined attention of the British Islanders; and it should not too much surprise us when, in our rambles through their country, we observe in them, concerning all matters of remote geography and ethnology, a depth, an amplitude, and a splendor of non-information, in the presence of which the alien observer is liable, unless carefully on his guard, to stand amazed and indeed convulsed. A fair instance of this sort of thing is mentioned by Mr. Henry Colman in his "European Life and Manners," published some twenty years ago. He speaks of being one day on the top of an omnibus in the Strand, and of seeing exhibited in a shop window a large block of ice from Wenham Lake: "I heard a well-dressed person, who sat on the other side of the driver, gravely inform him that this ice came from the West Indies." This truly brave flight of fancy will, perhaps, surprise us the less, if we recall what Harriet Martineau tells of the British speculative mania of 1825, when warming-pans from Birmingham were sent to Rio Janeiro, and skates from Sheffield were offered by the ship-load to a people who had never so much as seen ice. Moreover, these excited tradesmen of the North of England are not to be too severely dealt with by the reader; for no doubt they had as good an excuse for their hallucination as had the officials of their own government who, in the war they carried on against us in 1812, actually sent over to their little fleet in Lake Erie a supply of casks for fresh water, they supposing that the Great Lakes of America were simply respectable bodies of salt water, as perhaps they should have been. Not very unlike this, also, is the geographical paradox propounded in a poem published in London only a year or two ago—

a poem entitled " Stansfield, a Tragedy," by
Mr. Samuel Drake Roberts. It appears, on
the confession of Mr. Roberts himself, that
besides being a poet, he was in his earlier days
a traveller; and he herein gives us some rather
stirring reminiscences of the things he had observed in the latter capacity :

> " When younger, I have climbed the Alp and Pyrenee,
> Have mounted famed Olympus, and have gazed
> With wonderment and awe on Holy Sinai,
> And viewed with bated breath St. Lawrence thundering
> O'er Niagara's perpendicular crags,
> And felt the firm earth shake."

It would, of course, be deeply interesting if
we might be allowed to inquire exactly how
much " younger " Mr. Roberts really was at
the time when he beheld that astounding acrobatic exploit on the part of the St. Lawrence
River. His tragedy, by the way, is " dedicated to the memory of Shakespeare." Was
Mr. Roberts induced to heap this honor upon
the grave of Shakespeare, by a sort of intellectual kinship with that sublime genius, who,
sometimes soaring above what Mr. Punch
calls the " conventionalisms of geography,"
represented Bohemia as a maritime country,
and Verona as a city blessed with a seaport ?

Finally, as to matters ethnological or linguistic, I really should not like to be obliged to tell just how many times, during the past four years, I have been complimented on my somewhat remarkable escape from having the sable complexion so characteristic of my countrymen, as well as upon my apparent cleverness in mastering at least the rudiments of the noble language belonging to this kingdom. Nothing, however, in my own experience is half so delightful as that mentioned by Dr. Arthur Cleveland Coxe, now the Bishop of Western New York, who, in his little book on England, tells us how he once ran down from London to Devonshire, to visit a dear friend of his, the vicar of a parish there; and how, on his arrival, the children, who had heard that an American gentleman was coming to see them, were greatly disappointed because he had not a tawny face, was not wrapped in a blanket, had not feathers stuck in his hair, and had not even brought along his bows and arrows to lend to them while he stayed.

It would, perhaps, be churlish in us to quote too often Goldwin Smith's candid and indeed magnanimous explanation as to the true cause of his countrymen's lack of sympathy with us in our recent struggle for national existence; but this at least may be admitted, once for all, —that the height, depth, length, and breadth of the truth contained in that explanation can never be fully understood by any American without first coming over here and seeing for himself. As it would gratify us very much to be somewhat better known by our English cousins, so we may congratulate ourselves on one incidental benefit resulting from our late troubles: knowledge upon all things relating to America has become an object of rather greater curiosity to the English people than ever before. Many years ago, Southey wrote that in the neighborhood of Exeter were some conservative people who still spoke of Americans as " the rebels,"—the graphic and candid description of us to which, very naturally, they had become accustomed in the previous century. I think it just possible that by this time those good conservatives may have so far succumbed to Jacobinism and other vulgar novelties, as to adopt for us some new, though perhaps not much more complimentary, term. Of course, however, it would be presumptuous in us to expect so solid and tenacious a people as these to abandon all their ancient prejudices at once. We should be neither grieved nor indignant if, among many kind-hearted and hospitable English families, there should still remain for a while longer some incertitude as to the color or the native speech of the Americans; and even if, for one or two centuries to come, it be still a moot point whether the St. Lawrence River habitually run down-stream into its own gulf or up-stream " over Niagara's perpendicular crags," whether Massachusetts be not the principal city in Boston, and whether Chicago be not one of the most flourishing seaport towns of America, commanding, in fact, a picturesque view of the Pacific Ocean. We are not to be impatient with these noble-hearted people for not sooner grasping such far-off and complicated subjects. Besides, Rome was not built in a day. Let us have faith in the certain, if somewhat leisurely progress of human nature—and particularly of that sturdy branch of it represented by the inhabitants of these potent and self-centred isles.

1866.

AMERICAN REPUTATIONS IN ENGLAND

THERE is some analogy, as Charles Lamb once whimsically suggested to a friend of his who was travelling abroad, between the experience of being born into the world and that of being first landed in a foreign country. In either case, the stranger finds nearly every appeal to his five senses wondrously novel, startling, amusing; and the newly arrived traveller, like the newly arrived child, is apt to stare and listen and put out his hands at the most insignificant objects. But more impressive to the traveller than merely external novelties, is this realm of new ideas, new maxims, new whims, new prejudices, new reputations, into which he is introduced, with the inevitable obliteration of so many of those which he has just emigrated from. To an American coming to England, perhaps nothing gives a greater spiritual jar, nothing more startles him into realizing that he is actually abroad, than the discovery, constantly breaking upon him during the first weeks of his residence here, that, when he sailed away from America, he did indeed sail away from a whole hemisphere of personal authorities and reputations—from the principalities and powers of the literary, political, religious, and social world before which he had loyally bowed from his youth up. I think that, to any man, it would give at least a momentary shock to find, for the first time in his life, his references to illustrious names not understood, to august authorities not regarded, to the titular dignitaries of his native chess-board not saluted with deference or even with recognition.

As a matter of testimony upon this subject, perhaps I may be allowed to refer to some of my own experiences during a residence in England now extending over several years. I well remember the first decided shock of this kind which I received. It was soon after my arrival in London, and I was spending a part of the day with a literary man whose name, if I should mention it, would be recognized as a household word wherever the English language is spoken. I was showing to him and to a little circle of his friends my photograph album of American celebrities; and when we came to a certain face, they said, "Who is that?" I replied, "Oliver Wendell Holmes." "Who is he?" "Why, Dr. Holmes

—did you never hear of him?" "Never!" I confess that then, for the first time, I felt a little homesick. That word gave me, indeed, a sense of being "abroad." Before me, then, yawned the dreary distance from that dear spot which "there is no place like," with a vividness more painful than I had derived from all the three thousand farewells of the Atlantic, with all the taunts and jeers flung at us by "the countless laughter of its salt sea waves." Since then, that particular reputation has grown very rapidly in England; and, of course, even then there were here multitudes of the readers and admirers of the autocratic poet; but it was simply staggering to find cultivated men and women, eminent in English literature, too, who did not remember to have heard the name of Oliver Wendell Holmes!

Mr. Moncure Conway told me that he talked with a poor man in Venice who, he ascertained, had no knowledge of Daniel Webster, but was acquainted with the name and deeds of old John Brown. So I have found in England that, among the mass of the people—among those, for example, who make up a lecturer's audience at the literary and mechanics' institutes of the country—any reference to our great statesmen, jurists, and scholars of the time just gone, to Andrew Jackson, Calhoun, Webster, Clay, Story, Choate, Felton, requires explanation, while the mention of the names of philanthropists and reformers, especially of Garrison and Phillips, is generally caught up with instant appreciation and responded to with enthusiasm.

Certainly, for an American on this side of the sea there is the inevitable comic aspect to every experience of the sort; and when, here in London, glancing at his morning paper, he happens to read of "one A. T. Stewart,—a dry-goods person, we believe," or of "a certain Yankee who signs himself John S. C. Abbott," or of "Mr. Stephen A. Douglas, a capable negro, once a slave, and afterward an abolition orator," he feels that a real contribution has been made to the general stock of the gayety of nations. I think, however, that any countryman of mine who had grown up, as I did, under the omnipresence and the majesty of the renown of Daniel Webster, would be conscious of rather variegated sensations, should he happen to have a bit of experience at all like that which I am about to mention. A year ago, I arrived, at the close of a winter's day, in Plymouth—that noble old town on the south coast of England where our Pilgrim Fathers bade their last adieus to the cruel yet still beloved mother from whose frown they were fleeing. I went to an inn, was ushered into the coffee-room, and, while waiting for dinner, in the twilight I thought I saw hanging upon the opposite wall a portrait, life-size and done in oil, of Daniel Webster. It gave me a strange feeling full of pleasure, like hearing some familiar air of home, like seeing some well-known living face. I thought I must be mistaken, but, on rushing across the room, I found it was indeed a fine portrait of the great Daniel himself. Wondering how such a thing could have found its way into this quiet nook in one corner of England, when the waiter came in—a portly gentleman, dignified as a chief-justice or as one of the apostolic fathers—I asked him of whom that was the portrait. After some hesitation he said: "Ah, sir, I think I have heard master say it was some American gentleman or other. I will ask master, sir, if you wish." When he next entered he said: " I have asked master, sir; he does n't exactly remember the gentleman's name; he bought the picture at a sale; he thinks it is some American gentleman or other." And that is Fame—an old lady who seems to shudder at the Atlantic voyage. Just across the water, at the new Plymouth which the Pilgrim Fathers builded, how august a personage would have been evoked before every eye by that portrait! In the old Plymouth, however, it is merely the head of " some American gentleman or other." I sat there alone a long time over the coffee and in front of the bright fire, musing on the comedy of these solemn reputations of ours, and wondering whether the case with my country had been essentially changed since the year 1818, when Sydney Smith wrote in " The Edinburgh Review " : " There are no very prominent men at present in America, at least none whose fame is strong enough for exportation. Jefferson we believe is still alive. There is, or was, a Mr. Dwight who wrote some poems; and his baptismal name was Timothy."

We all find here a perpetual source of amusement in the very mixed apprehensions people have of the two most celebrated members of the Beecher family. Everybody knows Mrs. Stowe, and everybody calls her Mrs. Beecher-Stowe. Everybody knows Henry Ward Beecher, and nearly everybody calls him Mr. Beecher-Stowe. There is a confused idea of some very near relationship between these two individuals. It is generally stated that she is his wife, sometimes his daughter, occasionally his mother, seldom—what she is. I do not exaggerate in saying that, in nine cases out of ten, Henry Ward Beecher's name is by Englishmen enriched with the pleasing suffix of Stowe. Yet, a few weeks ago " The Times," in whose eyes he is of course a peculiarly endeared person, took quite the opposite way, and got the cart completely before the horse, by speaking of him as Mr. Beecher Ward!

Excluding, in these remarks, the small minority of English people who are really acquainted with our history and literature, I seldom meet with any one who seems to have heard of George W. Curtis, Dr. Holland, John G. Saxe, Colonel Higginson, Gail Hamilton, Bayard Taylor, Theodore Tuckerman, or Thomas B. Aldrich, whom we know so well, but whose names pronounced before a general English audience would be no more recognized than the names of so many under-secretaries of the tycoon. It is true that the books of some of them have had a considerable sale in England; but, in the first place, there is a large population of resident Americans here, who try to keep up an acquaintance with their country's authors; and, in the next place, there are a certain few English men and women who get and read all our best books as they appear. Upon the vast bulk of the population such names as these have as yet made no impression. Here and there their books are to be found; but such casual and sporadic circulation does not make fame or even reputation. The supreme American literary reputation in England is that of Longfellow. His renown has diffused itself into every household; his poems are in every drawing-room; he has more readers in England than any living English poet. His is the one only American literary name that may be mentioned in all companies with as much certainty of recognition as the name of Shakespeare, though even with Shakespeare's name it would not be safe to go below a certain tide-mark of English society. During the Shakespearian festivals in 1864, a London omnibus-driver, by whose side I had the temporary honor of a seat, whose daily journeys took him under the very walls of Apsley House and Buckingham Palace, gravely asked me, "Who is this fellow Shakespeare they 're making such a damned fuss about?" My impression is that, of American names, next to Longfellow in fame on British soil is Washington Irving, although an English lady of wealth and literary proclivities once inquired of me whether that was "the Irving who attracted so much notice as an eccentric preacher in London thirty years ago!" Perhaps next in renown to Longfellow and Irving, and in about the order given, are the names of Hawthorne, Emerson, Prescott, Lowell, Channing, Bryant, and Theodore Parker. I am surprised to find how many there are who do not know Whittier. It would be wrong to omit Elihu Burritt, who is everywhere known in England, and for whom there is an affectionate regard among multitudes of the purest and best. He has passed many years here; he has lectured in nearly every town and village; he has gone on foot through the whole length of the island; and by the simplicity, beauty, and amiability of his nature, by his supposed linguistic achievements, by his calm thinking, by his modest yet glowing speech, has not only made fame for himself, but has done much to elevate English estimates of the American character.

It is very probable that Americans who have made the tour of England may not be able altogether to verify my statements by their own experience, and especially may think that I have underrated the English reputation of some whom I have referred to. This is but natural. No two persons will have precisely the same experiences. Besides, mere tourists bring letters to the very people who are most interested in America, who know most about America, and in whose conversation these names are most familiarly used. It would be a mistake to infer that the English people in general have such an acquaintance with our literary names. But having repeatedly travelled up and down England, and having had in these journeys some glimpse of the interior of English life, as well as some chance of free conversation with vast numbers of English people, it is likely that my impressions are not what they would be were I seeing England as a tourist only. My duty in this paper, however, has been not to account for the impressions of others, but truthfully to relate my own.

It is with a melancholy interest that I look back over the growth of the English fame of Abraham Lincoln. During the first two years of my life here he was "the buffoon President," "the vulgar tyrant," "the brutal despot revelling in the woes of a race." As his name came naturally into some lectures on American topics which I was asked to give, I watched curiously the changes in the demonstrations which it excited. Except in very polite audiences it was always hissed. Even so late as the day on which we received the news of Mr. Lincoln's re-election, the mention of his name in a large audience convened in the very heart of London created a stormy susurration of hisses; and when the hisses provoked a retort of cheers, they rallied in tenfold intensity and won the night. His death has now changed all. During the autumn and winter after that event, laying the hand on the popular pulse in the same way, from Cornwall to Yorkshire, I found his name and praises welcomed with hearty tributes of applause.

In the "Scarlet Letter" occurs the just remark, that "it contributes greatly towards a man's moral and intellectual health to be brought into habits of companionship with individuals unlike himself, who care little for his pursuits, and whose sphere and abilities he must go out of himself to appreciate." May not a similar remark be made as to the advantages of companionship with those who care little for the personal reputations which have always awed us, for the august authorities with which we have been wont to fortify our speech, for some, at least, of the enthroned ones in literature with whose images we had filled the pantheon of our youthful homage? Yet it would be a rapture to get home again among the old names, and to take on once more the pleasant yoke of the old reputations.

1866.

THE END

INDEX

BY

WALTER HENRY OTTMAN, A.B.

Addison, Joseph, comment on London recalled, 3 ; quoted by John Bright, 178 ; cited, 257

"Adullamites," origin of term, 186

America, Mazzini's views concerning, 32 ; as viewed by humbler classes in foreign countries, 241 ; English hallucinations concerning, 277–295

Anne, Queen, 277, 278

Bacon, Francis, 13 ; effects of his speaking, 20

Balfour, Mrs. Clara Lucas, as a lecturer, 257, 268

Barré, Isaac, quoted, 283

Beales, Edmond, on House of Commons, 104, 105

Beecher, Henry Ward, 48, 162, 301 ; compared with Spurgeon, 52 ; farewell dinner to, 143 ; quoted, 214

Bismarck, Otto Edward Leopold, Prince von, 142, 162

Blanc, Jean Joseph Charles Louis, on John Bright, 182, 195

Boswell, James, cited, 3 ; characterizes House of Commons, 92

Braddock, Edward, his method of campaigning in America, 281, 282

Bright, John, 56, 59 ; describes Robert Lowe, 58 ; favors reform movements, 70 ; on House of Commons, 106 ; his opinion of Disraeli, 132 ; his opinion of Earl Russell, 153, 154 ; personal and political traits of, 155–161 ; his popularity, 155, 160, 161 ; compared with Charles Sumner, 156; likened to Wendell Phillips, 157; abuse of, 157, 158; personal appearance of, 158, 192; in House of Commons, 159, 195, 196; phases of his career, 162–170; early life, 162, 163; friendship with Cobden, 163; his constituencies, 164; obstacles to his success, 165; a political phenomenon, 167; his political doctrines, 168, 170; passages from his speeches, 169, 177, 178, 180, 181, 186-190, 193; as an orator, 171–199; his use of poetry, 177; on popular liberty in Europe, 177, 178; his perorations, 179; compared with Gladstone, 182; his common-sense, 183; his humor, 184-190; reference to seceding Liberals, 185; reply to Bulwer-Lytton, 186, 187; reference to Lord Derby, 187, 188; on Disraeli, 188; on the House of Lords, 189; as an iconoclast, 190; combativeness of, 192, 193; characteristics of his style, 193-195; Kinglake and Colman quoted concerning, 194; physical power of, 197; whom he represents, 198; as a public lecturer, 258

British Museum, 40, 153, 173; its hospitality, 124

Brougham, Henry, Lord, 162, 164; in House of Commons, 119; discussed, 137–143; premature announcement of his death, 138, 139; popular estimation of his character, 140; his merits, 141, 142; his eloquence, 141; Palmerston's opinion of, 141; helps establish the "Edinburgh Review," 142; character of his oratory, 175; his connection with the English lecture system, 255

Bulwer-Lytton, Sir Edward, 256; appearance of, 60; on English conversation, 174; Bright's reply to, 186, 187

Burke, Edmund, 40, 95, 256; likened to Gladstone, 66; to Brougham, 141; character of his oratory, 174

Byron, George Roel Gordon, quoted, 83, 216, 217; "English Bards and Scotch Reviewers," 142

Canning, George, 165; in Parliament of 1827, 72, 73; opposed by English patricians, 75; compared with Gladstone, 85; opposed by Brougham, 141

Carbonari, the, Mazzini allied with, 27

INDEX 309

Cardiff, 229, 234; characterized, 223; visit to American consulate at, 234-241

Carlyle, Thomas, on House of Commons, 100, 101; speech by, at Edinburgh, 173

Channing, William Ellery, 303

Chatham, Earl of (William Pitt), 48, 95, 131, 250; compared with Gladstone, 85

Cobbett, William, cited, 259

Cobden, Richard, 65, 163, 164, 166, 198, 201; attacked by English patricians, 76; his friendship for John Bright, 163, 168, 192; cited, 193, 289

Coleridge, Samuel Taylor, 184; "Home and Grave of," 216-222; his personal appearance, 221

Colman, Henry, quoted, 194, 195, 291

Commons, House of, J. S. Mill in, 54-63, 107; characterized, 54; basis of representation in, 66; debates in, 69; ladies' gallery in, 82, 99, 107; appearance of members of, 82; its local habitation, 92-101; Boswell's opinion of, 92; approach to, 96; physical appointments of, 96, 97; distribution of seats in, 97, 98; galleries in, 99; its personal composition, 102-110; expense of election to, 104; Beales's opinion of, 105; Disraeli's opinion of, 105; tendency to class legislation in, 105, 106; Bright's accusation regarding, 106; courtesy in, 106-110, 114-121; its manners, 111-121; its supremacy in the empire, 112; compared with French and American legislatures, 113, 114; peculiar customs in, 119; Bishop Coxe characterizes, 160; its independence of the Crown, 211

Conway, Moncure Daniel, 19; letter from Mazzini to, cited, 32; speaks on American question, 38; cited, 298

Cooper, James Fenimore, on the manners of the Anglo-Saxon race, 108; his conversation with Lord Holland, 290

Coxe, Arthur Cleveland, cited, 160, 293

Crimean War, John Bright's opposition to, 164

Cromwell, Oliver, 95, 148, 167; quoted, 247

Croquill, Alfred, his portrait of Disraeli, 129

Curran, John Philpot, 197

Dawson, George, as a lecturer, 260
De Quincey, Thomas, 111
Derby, Earl of, 59, 162, 164, 256; opposed to the reform bill of 1866, 70; his government characterized by John Bright, 187, 188
Dickens, Charles, as a lecturer, 253
Disraeli, Benjamin, 59, 162, 165; opposes reform bill of 1866, 70; his manners in the House, 107, 125; discussed, 122-136; his ancestors, 122, 123; his personal appearance, 125-127; solitary appearance of, 126; his artificiality, 128; his Mephistophelian temper, 128; his talents, 128, 129; principal works by, 129, 133-135; his early life, 129; appearance as a young man, 129; his early political career, 130; stigmatizes O'Connell, 130; obtains seat in Parliament, 130; his first speech, 130, 131; attacks Sir Robert Peel, 131; high character of his speeches, 132; his genius, 132, 133, 165; his literary works discussed, 133-135; his inconsistency, 136; compared with John Bright, 185; Bright's reference to, 188, 189; as a lecturer, 258
Disraeli, Isaac, father of Benjamin, 122; sent to Amsterdam, 123; writes poem against commerce, 123; publishes "The Abuse of Satire," 123; friendship with Pye, 123; principal works of, 124
Douglas, Stephen Arnold, 299

Elliott, Ebenezer, 64
Emerson, Ralph Waldo, 303; cited, 108
England, "Isle of the Future," 64; changing system of legislation in, 68, 69; aristocracy in, 167; liberty in her colonies, 177; cost of royalty, 202; Beecher's reference to, 214; characteristics of crime in, 243; rough sports in, 244; frankness of her people, 246; Dr. Johnson a typical citizen of, 248; her conditions after Waterloo, 261; popularizing of knowledge in, 261-264; class system in, 263, 264; American reputations in, 296-306

Family position, as an element in English politics, 145

Fawcett, Henry, associated with Lord Brougham, 142
Fielding, Henry, cited, 11
Fox, Charles James, 95; Brougham a successor of, 141; cited, 175
Fox, George, 191
Francis, George Henry, his opinion of Earl Russell, 146

Garibaldi, Giuseppe, in London, 47
Garrison, William Lloyd, 163, 168, 299
George III., 200, 279, 282
Gibbon, Edward, on hearing a report of his own death, 140
Gladstone, William Ewart, 162, 164, 165, 168, 169, 258; his indefatigability in Parliament 55, 59, 60; his appearance in the House, 55, 82, 107; proposes reform in parliamentary representation, 66; supports the measure, 70; speech on reform cited, 70, 71; in defeat, 72-81; leader of Parliament, 73; opposition to, 74, 75; Mill's characterization of, 74; causes of opposition to, 75-78; offence of, 76; earnestness of, 77; popular enthusiasm for, 79-81; accusation against, 82-91; his temperament, 83; Tory papers on, 84; "New York Times" on, 85; compared with other leaders, 85; his equanimity and courtesy, 86; Thomas Hughes quoted concerning, 87; John F. Maguire on, 88, 89; temper of, 89; listens to attacks upon himself, 90; eulogy of, 90, 91; reception of his speeches by House of Commons, 119; his friendliness with members of House, 126; compared with Bright, 182
Grant, General, 142, 162; effects of his victories, 65
Grattan, Henry, 95
Grote, George, quoted, 212

Hampden, John, 95
Hannay, James, quoted, 290
Hansard, Luke, 119; "Debates," 130, 158
Hardy, John, cited, 195
Hastings, Warren, Sheridan's philippic against, 93; trial of, 95

Hawthorne, Nathaniel, 303; cited, 47, 260
Helps, Arthur, cited, 209
Herbert, George, quoted by John Bright, 177
Hill, Rowland, 37; Sheridan's remark regarding, 49
Hogarth, William, 122
Holmes, Oliver Wendell, 297
Hook, Theodore Edward, cited, 247
Horner, Francis, 142
Howitt, William and Mary, their home in Highgate, 216–219
Hughes, Thomas, 168; addresses citizens of London, 7; on Mr. Gladstone, 87; associated with Lord Brougham, 142
Hume, Joseph, Palmerston's remark concerning, 118; endorses Disraeli, 130

Irving, Edward, 33
Irving, Washington, 303

Jefferson, Thomas, 301
Jeffrey, Francis, associated with Lord Brougham, 142
Johnson, Samuel, on size of London, 3, 4; Isaac Disraeli visits, 122; on dogs, 137; cited, 157; on quotations, 176; a representative Briton, 248, 249
Jonson, Ben, his account of Bacon's oratory, 20
Juvenal, quoted, 213

Kelly, Fitzroy, 59
Kinglake, Alexander William, on oratory of John Bright, 194
Kinkel, Johann Gottfried, quoted, 267
Knight, Charles, quoted, 166
Knox, John, 48; cited, 194

Lamb, Charles, cited, 113; his visits to Coleridge, 222
Latimer, Hugh, 48
Layard, Austen Henry, 119

Lecturing, popular, 253-276; requirements for, 254, 272; how viewed in England, 255-259; English and American systems compared, 261, 263, 274, 275; financial returns from, 265-270; leading lecturers in America, 265; in England, 267-270; its present condition in England, 271-276

Liberals, the, 64-99; prostration of (1860-1865), 65; their attitude toward American crisis, 66; prospects of their cause, 75

Lincoln, Abraham, 142, 205, 235; his reputation in England, 305

London, 1-12; not known by its inhabitants, 1; its cosmopolitan character, 2, 3; Boswell's estimation of, 4; population by decades (1801-1861), 4; its magnitude, 5, 6; day and night populations of, 6; anxiety caused by its rapid growth, 7; need for purer air, 7; houses and streets in, 8; consumption of gas, fuel, and provisions, 9; professional men in, 10; churches, 10; "all roads lead up to," 11; the intellectual and moral capital of the globe, 11

Longfellow, Henry Wadsworth, his reputation in England, 302

Lords, House of, 286; a constitutional fiction, 112; characterized by John Bright, 189

Louis Napoleon (Napoleon III.), 142, 162

Lowe, Robert, John Bright describes, 58; debates with John Stuart Mill, 58; opposes reform bill of 1866, 70; sociability in the House, 126; secedes from Liberals, 185

Lowell, James Russell, 303

Macaulay, Thomas Babington, in House of Commons, 70; describes New Palace Yard, 93; cited, 148

Macchiavelli, Niccolo, 245

Maguire, John Francis, "Biography of Father Mathew," by 87; letter by, quoted, 88, 89

Martineau, Harriet, "History of the Peace," quoted, 72; cited, 119, 169, 291

Masson, David, a speaker for John Stuart Mill's election, 19

Mazzini, Giuseppe, 24–32 ; health and physical appearance, 25 ; fascinating presence, 26 ; his physical endurance, 26 ; his literary activity, 26 ; early career, 27, 28 ; settles in London, 28 ; his fearless character, 30 ; his tenderness, 30, 31 ; his letter to Moncure Conway, 32 ; views on America, 32

Mill, John Stuart, 162, 168, 169 ; as a stump speaker, 13–23 ; his candidacy for Parliament, 13–15 ; a friend to America, 15 ; his personal appearance, 18, 19, 57 ; a phrenological inventory of, 18 ; his speech and manner, 19–21, 60 ; his learning, 21, 58 ; elected to Parliament, 23 ; as member of House of Commons, 54–63 ; speeches on various subjects, 56–58 ; argues for the reform bill, 59 ; on the tax on malt, 59–62; probable effect of his words on the public, 63 ; favors reform bill of 1866, 70 ; characterization of Gladstone by, 74, 85 ; "below the gangway," 98, 99 ; remarks of Edmond Beales to, 105 ; manners in the House, 107, 126

Miller, Hugh, opinion of London cited, 1

Milton, John, his salutation of Shakespeare, 3

Molesworth, William Nassau, "History of Reform Bill," by, quoted, 152

Montesquieu, Baron de, cited, 202

Moore, Thomas, a friend of Earl Russell, 147

Motley, John Lothrop, cited, 141

Napoleon Bonaparte, 142, 261 ; quoted, 213

Nelson, Horatio, Lord, quoted, 256

Newcastle, William Cavendish, Duke of, 280

Newman, Francis, 168

Newton, Sir Isaac, 25

Noel, Baptist Wriothesley, 33–41 ; early popularity of, 33, 34 ; advantages of aristocratic position of, 34 ; his personal attractiveness, 34 ; his creed, 35 ; lines of work pursued by, 35 ; withdraws from Established Church, 36 ; unites with Baptist denomination, 37 ; at Finsbury Chapel, 38 his many-sided interests, 38 ; his attitude toward America, 38, 39 ; manner of speech of, 39 ; success as a pastor, 39, 40 ; extensive literary activity of, 40 ; important publications of, 40, 41

North, Frederick, Lord, 280

O'Connell, Daniel, his remarks in House of Commons cited, 120 ; his relations with Disraeli, 130, 131

Oratory, how estimated in England, 171, 174

Otis, James, quoted, 283

Owen, Robert Dale, lends money to the Duke of Kent, 200

Pakington, Sir John Somerset, 125

Palmerston, Lord, *see* Temple, Henry J.

Peel, Sir Robert, Disraeli's attacks on, 131, 132 ; compared with Earl Russell, 150

Phillips, Wendell, 299 ; his resemblance to John Bright, 157 ; character of his oratory, 175

Pitt, William, *see* Chatham, Earl of

Pitt, William, son of preceding, 40 ; compared with Gladstone, 85

Pluck of the English people, 242-252 ; its celebrity, 242; admiration felt for, 243 ; as manifested by children, 249-252

Plutarch, 117

Plymouth, 299, 300

Poe, Edgar Allan, 290

Prescott, William Hickling, 303

Prior, James, cited, 256

Prior, Matthew, quoted, 213

" Punch," 292 ; on Earl Russell, 47 ; on John Bright, 173

Pye, Henry James, befriends Isaac Disraeli, 123

Reform movement, 64-71 ; an echo of Lee's surrender, 64 ; proposed by Gladstone, 66 ; its main provisions, 66 ; probable results of the movement, 67, 68 ; its reception, 67 ; debates upon, 69 ; leading opponents and supporters of, 70; Gladstone's speech on, cited, 70, 71; its eventual success prophesied, 71

Revolution, French, a historic corollary of the American Revolution, 64

Roberts, Samuel Drake, quoted, 292

Robertson, Frederick William, attacks on, 37

Roebuck, John Arthur, in House of Commons, 126; remarks concerning Earl Russell cited, 148

Rome, 3, 200; Republic of, 28; orators of, discussed, 116, 117

Rousseau, Jean Jacques, 111

Russell, Earl, 47, 70, 162, 164; discussed, 144-154; his popularity in England, 144; advantages from family position of, 145; education of, 145, 146; early attachment to human rights, 146; early political career, 147; principles supported by, 147; his connection with the reform bill of 1832, 147, 148; decay of his popularity, 149; fame eclipsed by that of Palmerston, 149; failure in diplomacy and finance, 149, 150; compared with Peel and Palmerston, 150; his respect for public opinion, 150; his attitude toward the American Civil War, 151; his oratorical abilities, 151; readiness at repartee, 152; chief literary works of, 153; his political integrity, 153; John Bright's opinion of, 153, 154

" Russell's Purge," term applied to reform bill of 1832, 148

Schiller, Johann Christoph Friedrich von, cited, 29

Scott, Benjamin, city chamberlain of London, 7

Scott, Sir Walter, quoted, 224, 225

Shakespeare, William, 172, 292, 303; Milton's salutation of, 3

Shenstone, William, quoted by Bright, 187

Sheridan, Richard Brinsley, his remark concerning Rowland Hill, 59; at trial of Hastings, 93, 95; quoted, 180

Sidney, Philip, quoted, 84

Smith, Adam, 13

Smith, Goldwin, 168, 293

Smith, Sydney, his opinion of Macaulay, 2 ; regarding English gentlemen, 109 ; associated with Lord Brougham 142; on English audiences, 174 ; quoted, 301
Society for the Diffusion of Knowledge, 261
Solinus, Caius Julius, quoted, 252
Somers, John, 95
Southey, Robert, cited, 294
Spurgeon, Charles Haddon, 33 ; sermon on "Baptismal Regeneration," 38 ; attitude of other preachers toward, 43 ; growing success of, 44 ; size of his audiences, 45 ; attitude of audiences toward, 45 ; his personal characteristics, 46, 47 ; his fluency and purity of speech, 48 ; accused of vulgarisms, 48 ; his manners, 49 ; regarding committees, 49 ; his earnestness, 50 ; likened to Whitefield, 51, 53 ; character of his sermons commonplace, 51 ; compared with Beecher, 52 ; his loyalty to the Baptist denomination, 53
Stanhope, James, his methods likened to those of Mazzini, 30
Story, Joseph, 298
Stowe, Mrs. Harriet Beecher, 301
Sumner, Charles, compared with John Bright, 156, 162, 168 ; as a lecturer, 258
Swift, Jonathan, quoted, 83
Sydney, Algernon, 95

Tacitus, Cornelius, cited, 252
Taylor, Bayard, 302
Taylor, Peter, member of House of Commons, 105
Temple, Henry John, Viscount Palmerston, 76, 89 ; a political Sadducee, 77 ; his reference to Joseph Hume, 118 ; describes Brougham, 141 ; his character as a statesman, 149 ; compared with Earl Russell, 150
Tennyson, Alfred, Lord, 207 ; a recluse, 14 ; cited, 213, 215
Thackeray, William Makepeace, 25 ; as a lecturer, 253
Thompson, George, his acquaintance with America, 39 ; member of Parliament, 58
Thornbury, Walter, cited, 10, 11

"Times, The," 195; describes Earl Russell, 150; criticises the Queen, 212; on Beecher, 302

"Times, The New York," its remarks on Gladstone cited, 85

Townshend, Charles, 280

Tuckerman, Theodore, 302

Victoria, Alexandrina, Queen of England, 79, 80, 167, 278; her early economy, 201; her income, 203; her personal influence, 206-210; American and English opinions of her compared, 207, 208; loyalty of English people to, 210; her actual power, 211; wars during her reign, 214; her renown for wisdom and goodness, 215

Vincent, Henry, 260

Wales, suffrage in, 66; male population of, 67; a Sunday in, 223-233; popularizing of knowledge in, 262

Washington, George, 142, 205, 235

Webster, Daniel, 235, 298-300; character of his oratory, 175

Westminster Abbey, 43, 93

Westminster Hall, 80; described, 93, 94

Whitefield, George, 33, 48; Bacon's remark concerning, 50, 51; Spurgeon compared with, 53; character of his oratory, 175

Whittier, John Greenleaf, 303

Wilberforce, William, 40; cited, 109

Wilks, Washington, cited, 143

Wordsworth, William, quoted, 263

AMERICAN HISTORY.

THE LITERARY HISTORY OF THE AMERICAN REVOLUTION: 1763-1783.

By Moses Coit Tyler, Professor of American History in Cornell University, and author of "A History of American Literature during the Colonial Times," etc. Two volumes, sold separately. Large 8°. Each . . $3 00

Vol. I.—1763-1776; Vol. II.—1776-1783.

"Professor Tyler's newest work is rich, stimulating, informing, and delightful. And it is not only fascinating itself, but it is a luminous guide into the whole abundant, varied, and alluring field of our revolutionary literature: poetry, belles-lettres, biography, history, travel, and crackling controversy."—GEORGE W. CABLE, in *Current Literature*.

"A work certain to be welcomed by students of history throughout the world."—*New York Sun*.

A HISTORY OF AMERICAN LITERATURE DURING THE COLONIAL TIME.

By Moses Coit Tyler, Professor of American History, Cornell University. New edition revised, in two volumes. Volume I.—1607-1676. Volume II.—1676-1765.
Each $2 50
Agawam edition, 2 vols. in one. 8°, half leather. 3 00

"It must be a satisfaction to you to know that your work on the Colonial Period has been so well done that it will never need to be done over again."—LONGFELLOW to the Author.

COMPARATIVE ADMINISTRATIVE LAW.

An Analysis of the Administrative Systems National and Local, of the United States, England, France, and Germany. By F. J. Goodnow, Professor of Administrative Law in Columbia College. Part I.—Organization. Part II.—Legal Relations. 2 vols. 8°, cloth, each . $2 50

"We regard these two volumes as the most important contribution to political science . . . which has been published in this country, we will not undertake to say for how long."—*The Independent*.

"A work of great learning and profound research . . . remarkable alike for analytical power and lucidity of method . . . unique and of permanent excellence."—*New York Tribune*.

"A wealth of research and illustration of which Germany herself might be proud, though the manner is all too clear and practical for Germany."—*London Observer*.

G. P. PUTNAM'S SONS

NEW YORK   LONDON

WORKS BY THEODORE ROOSEVELT.

The Winning of the West.

Four volumes. Each volume is complete in itself and is sold separately. 8°, cloth, with maps. Each . . $2 50

"A story full of interesting incidents, which never grows dull from the first page to the last; written after much research, and with impartial soberness; an admirable contribution to the history of America."—*London Spectator*.

Hunting Trips of a Ranchman.

Sketches of Sport on the Northern Cattle Plains. With 27 full-page wood engravings and 8 smaller engravings, from designs by A. B. Frost, R. Swain Gifford, J. C. Beard, Fannie E. Gifford, and Henry Sandham. Bevelled boards, 8° $3 00

"One of those distinctively American books which ought to be always welcomed as contributing distinctly to raise the literary prestige of the country all over the world."—*New York Tribune*.

The Wilderness Hunter.

With an account of the Big Game of the United States, and its chase with Horse, Hound, and Rifle. With illustrations by Remington, Frost, Sandham, Eaton, Beard, and others. 8° $3 50

"Written by a mighty hunter, also a naturalist as well as a sportsman, a close observer as well as a sure shot; not John Burroughs himself could write more interestingly of the sights and sounds of the wilderness."—*Philadelphia Telegraph*.

The Naval War of 1812.

Or, The History of the United States Navy during the last war with Great Britain. To which is appended an account of the Battle of New Orleans. 4th edition, 8°, cloth $2 50

"The volume is an excellent one in every respect, and shows in so young an author the best promise for a good historian—fearlessness of statement, caution, endeavor to be impartial, and a brisk and interesting way of telling events."—*N. Y. Times*.

G. P. PUTNAM'S SONS, NEW YORK AND LONDON.

www.ingramcontent.com/pod-product-compliance
Lightning Source LLC
Chambersburg PA
CBHW021155230426
43667CB00006B/413